Elusive Culture

SUNY series, Identities in the Classroom
Deborah P. Britzman, editor

Elusive Culture

*Schooling, Race, and Identity
in Global Times*

Daniel A. Yon

State University of New York Press

Published by
State University of New York Press

© 2000 State University of New York

For information, address the State University of New York Press
State University Plaza, Albany, NY 12246

Marketing by Anne M. Valentine • Production by Bernadine Dawes

Library of Congress Cataloging-in-Publication Data

Yon, D. A.
    Elusive Culture: schooling, race, and identity in global times /
Daniel A. Yon.
        p.   cm. — (SUNY series, identities in the classroom)
    Includes bibliographical references (p.   ) and index.
    ISBN 0-7914-4481-3 (hc. : alk. paper). — ISBN —7914-4482-1 (pbk.
: alk. paper)
        1. Educational anthropology Case studies. 2. Critical pedagogy
Case studies. 3. High school students—Psychology Case studies.
4. Ethnicity Case studies. I. Title. II. Series
LB45-Y66 2000   99-31134
306.43—dc21   CIP

1 2 3 4 5 6 7 8 9 10

For my nieces and nephews

Contents

Foreword

Elusive Culture is based on Daniel Yon's long and detailed ethnographic study of how race and identity are negotiated amongst the culturally and racially diverse students of Maple Heights, an inner-city secondary school located in metropolitan Toronto. These young people are drawn from every conceivable national, linguistic, racial, ethnic, and cultural background. The unusual term "elusive" is applied to ways cultural processes work in the school. The main purpose of the book is to "engage the fluidity that marks the sets of relationships through which culture, race, and identity are made."

Traditionally, a school like Maple Heights is often described in terms of the loss of cultural identity. Kids whose backgrounds are so mixed-up and diverse must, it is assumed, be confused about who they are and where they belong. In conventional pedagogic analysis, cultural diversity and identity fragmentation are usually directly linked to behavioral problems, low self-esteem, and poor academic attainment at school. It is this "cover story" that Daniel Yon's ethnography sets out to challenge. The conventional account, he argues, is grounded in certain (often unstated) core suppositions: that identity arises from inside the person—the inner core of the self—and is a fixed and stable structure; that culture is unitary, essentialist and all-encompassing. This is the view of identity and culture that underpins much of the theory and practice of multi-culturalism, where cultural belongingness is conceived as total: saturating our lives in a homogeneous way and scripting them from end to end.

Yon's ethnography not only shows us otherwise, it gives us a richly textured, more complex and "elusive" sense of how culture works and how identity is produced and negotiated when neither is fixed nor stable. Ethnography is, of course, a fieldwork methodology well developed in anthropology. It has been widely adapted to more contemporary institutional situations, including classroom studies. Its great merit is that it shows in detail and in depth how subjective meanings mediate the micro-social processes involved in everyday social life in something approaching their natural settings. Precisely because of their grounding in the specific and the particular, ethnographies are hard to generalize or to theorize. They enrich—rather than produce—concepts and theories.

In this case, however, the ethnographic approach has both a descriptive and conceptual payoff. Daniel Yon wishes to test a whole new way of theorizing culture and identity, as well as exemplify in textured detail how those theories work in a real-life situation. But to do that he has to set his whole enterprise in a new conceptual frame or map. In his opening chapter, he draws extensively on recent critical cultural theory, on post-colonial studies, and post-structural writing to inform the ethnographic concepts he then deploys. In turn, the fieldwork gives much of the recent challenging but rather speculative theorizing a subtle and concrete grounding.

What he is able to demonstrate again and again in the analysis he offers of his observations, conversations, interviews, and group discussions with his students, is that culture in our modern urban settings is best understood discursively as an "open text." His participants treat it, not as doctrine or *doxa*, but as a *repertoire of meanings*. Identity is not already "there"; rather, it is a production, emergent, in process. It is situational—it shifts from context to context. The identity passionately espoused in one public scenario is more ambiguously and ambivalently "lived" in private. Its contradictions are negotiated, not "resolved." Meaning is essential to this whole process of identity-production, but is always an open weave to be reinflected and reappropriated. The body itself, which is so much "at stake" in contemporary youth cultures, does not serve to give an essential and material grounding to identity. It, too, is handled like a text—to be read (by oneself and well as by others). Far from the traditional "culture of origin" that provides an anchor and point of reference in this fluid world, identities are constantly reworked with meaning and images drawn from the rapidly changing circuits of popular culture. Accordingly, the school appears here less as an institutional site with structural properties and more as a "discursive space." There is indeed what Yon calls "a passion for identity." There is considerable personal and social investment in its positionalities. What there is *not* is a passion for identity to *stay the same*.

This applies even to what may sometimes appear to be the most essentialized and well-grounded of identity categories—those related to so-called "race." There are a hundred different ways in which the students of Maple Heights live or produce the category "blackness": the multiplicity of its instantiations helps to unsettle its apparently monolithic character. Its boundaries overlap and diverge. Its content is filled out with the help of a very wide field of reference, each definition shifting its meaning. Even racialized categories—which many regard as among the most rigid of classifications—seem to generate multiple forms of belongingness.

The mistake would be to imagine that, because the boundaries have become so fluid, the category has ceased to matter. Or because identity is more open-ended, it has ceased to matter very much. This book shows that quite the reverse is the case. The proliferation of meanings and identities in late modernity make the question of identity matter *more* not less.

The evidence and argument of this book is modestly presented, but its implications are wide-ranging and of critical importance. It has much to say to teachers and administrators, to policy makers and cultural analysts, to students and researchers; indeed to anyone in the community who is willing to unravel the elusive puzzle that is the cultural complexity with which our metropolitan and cosmopolitan reality confronts us today.

Stuart Hall
London, October 1999

Acknowledgments

Some of the issues and concerns that emerge in this book—concerns with migrations, diaspora, globalization and transnationalism; the shifting contours of race, culture and identity; debates about culture, cultural hybridity and creolization; about roots, "routes" and questions of representation, to mention a few—have become hotly contested subjects as we move from one millennium into another and as we attempt to reflect upon these times. Having made my home in more than one place around the world, these themes are not only academic for me, they are also personal. The experiences, encounters, and conversations with friends to whom I am very grateful over the course of my own "routes"—which link places as diverse St. Helena, England, Zimbabwe, and Canada—have no doubt affected the reflections I bring to this work.

This book began as a doctoral dissertation, and I express deep thanks to my dissertation supervisor, Frances Henry, and committee members Malcolm Blincow and Margaret Rodman, professors in the Department of Anthropology, York University, as well as Deborah Britzman, professor in the Faculty of Education, for their valuable advice, guidance, and support. I am very grateful for the Canadian Commonwealth Scholarship that was awarded to me for my doctoral studies and that helped fund the initial research upon which both my dissertation and this book are based.

It would not have been possible to produce this book without the support and cooperation of all those at Maple Heights, the school where my research was undertaken. The ethics of research do not allow me to address any of these people by name, but I thank the school principal, vice principals, support staff, teachers, and students for allowing me to become a part of the school for the year that I was there. Special thanks to the students for the confidence and trust they invested in me, for the relationships that were formed, and for making the whole process of research a pleasurable experience.

The title of this book was born in a warm restaurant on Bloor Street, Toronto, on a very cold February night. In conversation with Deborah Britzman about the possible transition from doctoral dissertation to book, I declared my interest in trying to capture the elusiveness of culture (and the other concepts that make it intelligible) as my contribution to the on-going debates about culture and education. "There's a title!" Deborah interjected. And so "Elusive Culture" it came to be. I express my sincere thanks to Deborah for inviting me to be a part of her series, Identities in the Classroom. I have benefitted greatly from her brilliant mind and her generosity of spirit. My thanks to State University of New York Press for facilitating the production. Thanks also to Bronwen Low and Colette Granger, for copyediting and proofreading and to Tim Low for help in citation searches and indexing

I am privileged to be part of a lively and interesting community of scholars and students at York University and to have lovely and supportive friends here and beyond. Rather than risk leaving anyone out, I extend my general but warm thanks to all.

Finally, but not least, I thank my mother and family, who are far from where I write, for their love and unspoken but solid support.

1

Mapping the Field

Observers of the twentieth and the onset of the twenty-first century will note how these times are distinguished by a peculiar passion for identity: identities made around nation, community, ethnicity, race, religion, gender, sexuality, and age; identities premised on popular culture and its shifting sets of representational practices; identities attached to fashion and new imagined lifestyles, to leisure and work, and to the mundane and the exotic; identities made in relation to place and displacement, to community and to a sense of dispersal, to "roots" as well as "routes." This book is an engagement with the passionate question of identity in what I call "global times." It explores these questions of identity and related questions of culture through an ethnographic study of the dynamics played out by youth in an urban high school in the city of Toronto. I will call this school Maple Heights.[1]

Returning to the passion for identity, and the passion of identity, observers might also note a peculiar paradox of these times. On the one hand the closing decade of the twentieth century is marked by openings and possibilities for reaching out across differences, by transnational and post-national identities that accompany aspiration toward global citizenship. Challenges are made to the previously taken for granted assumptions about what one's place of birth has to do with the ways identities are made. But on the other hand these times are also marked by closures, identity politics, social aggression, and civic strife. While new and improved forms of technology enhance rapid movements and flows of communication and bring about the global village, new boundaries, identities, and exclusions (built upon racist practices, ethnic absolutism and nationalism) reassert restrictions on the movements of others.[2] Furthermore, while the conditions of displacement and migration are celebrated by some, millions more are affected by persecution, war, and poverty. What these contradictory and conflicting conditions suggest is that identities are shaped by context and history. Identity experimentation and imagined possibilities are free floating and a matter of choice for some, but they are also the results of encounters with boundaries of exclusion for others.

The passion for identity takes shape as assumptions about sameness or difference between selves and communities are brought into question and people begin to reflect upon who they are or worry about what they are becoming.[3] Such a passion is evident in intense academic debates, popular talk shows, and everyday conversations. Since talk of identity merges with the practices of identity, identities cannot be separated from the knowledge and representations which they express and repress. Nor is identity beyond what Giddens describes as the "double hermeneutics."[4] This is a reference to how those we research may internalize the language of the researcher and talk and act through the concepts and meanings that language produces. There is, in other words, an intimate relationship between the various discourses and representations of identities and how identities are made and performed. But this observation does not mean that individuals are passive objects or dupes of identity trends and fashions. Instead it draws attention to the self-reflexivity entailed in identity construction, to how individuals mediate and reflect upon these trends and make them their own. People act upon knowledge, even as it acts upon them. For understanding this process the concept *discourse* is of special importance, and central to our ethnographic study of the encounters of youth and identity at Maple Heights.

In popular usage "discourse" refers simply to conversation and writing. It is used both as a noun, designating a treatise on a subject, and as a verb meaning to speak or to write. What is important here is the intimate relationship between noun and verb, between knowledge and its actions. In thinking about this relationship I am influenced by the large and established field of discourse analysis and discourse theory.[5] In this field discourse is defined as a collection of statements and ideas that produces networks of meanings. These networks structure the possibilities for thinking and talking and become the conceptual framework and the classificatory models for mapping the world around us. Discourse shapes how we come to think and produce new knowledge, and facilitates shared understandings and engagements. Important to note, however, is that even as discourse facilitates thought and actions it may also work to constrain, as it sets up the parameters, limits, and blind spots of thinking and acting. This recalls Michel Foucault's notion of *power/knowledge*, by which discourse disciplines subjects even as it positions them and facilitates in the social world.[6] In other words, discourse is both enabling and constraining.

Clearly, power is central to discourse. But power must not be thought about in this context as something that one has or does not have. It exceeds the Marxian sense of power as that which can be seized or that from which one is alienated.[7] Power is neither simply about material ownership nor about making relationships to what Bourdieu calls "cultural capital."[8] It is not synonymous with the decision-making apparatus of institutions and government. Instead, the power of discourse is productive, and works in multiple, multidirectional ways. For example, the power that is inherent in identity categories such as *woman, man, youth, Black,* and *White,* structures the possibilities for acting in terms of socially intelligible subjectivities or what it means to be one or more of these categories. The categories, in other words, can be categories of empowerment. But even as they enable and empower subjects, such identity categories also hold the potential to constrain by prescribing and restricting what it means to *be* woman, man, youth, Black, White, and so on. To consider such conflicted possibilities, notions of both power and discourse must be dynamic and include an understanding of how constraint is also productive. This will become clearer later when we see individuals acting with and acting against the power effects of identity categories and knowledge.

The concept *discourse* alerts us to what language does, and to how it produces and situates individuals. Such a critical engagement with language and its effects also asks us to think about how certain meanings become common sense—how specific discourses become "authoritative" or "dominant."[9] For example, let us take our concept of culture. Culture is often popularly talked and written about as a set of stable and timeless attributes that distinguish groups. It is imagined in terms of what anthropologist Clifford Geertz, following Durkheim, refers to as the "webs of significance" through which people make sense of their worlds and those of others.[10] This specific understanding of culture is about histories, traditions, shared beliefs, and folklore. These visual, oral, and written forms of cultural representations are seen as the property of individuals and groups, prompting talk of "your" culture, "my" culture, "dominant" culture, "minority" cultures, and so on. Culture is here viewed as a product to be received and passed on. So dominant is this specific discourse that alternative notions of culture that challenge the very idea of culture as a site of identity may be difficult to imagine. In this book, the concept *elusive culture* responds to this challenge. The book is an attempt to gesture toward a more open and pervasive view of culture, which is not only a product or a set of attributes that can be claimed and neatly recorded, but more significantly, a process that is ongoing. Individuals participate in the process of culture, not just in webs of tradition, but, as we shall see in subsequent chapters, also in surprising movements and ways that may exceed the culturally given or expected.

As I map out the conceptual field for the ethnography of Maple Heights, there is a tension within my attempts to delineate the concepts of culture, race, and identity. In dealing with each separately below, I draw attention to their conceptual distinction. After all, these are specific words and concepts that address different social phenomena. However, it is equally important to bear in mind the relationship between these concepts, their discourses, and their convergences in academic and popular discourses. As this study of Maple Heights demonstrates, race may function as culture, culture as identity, and identity as race. Such convergences lend elusive qualities to the categories. I stress convergences because culture, race, and identity are often talked about as if they are stable, bounded entities rather than slippery and shifting.

Discourses of Culture, Identity, and Race

Culture

While undertaking the research for this book, I came across a relatively short UNESCO publication entitled *Voices in a Seashell: Education, Culture and Identity*. The publication is the outcome of a seminar on indigenous cultures and schooling in the South Pacific. I quote from this work because the particular discourse of culture that it reproduces is one that a notion of elusive culture can critically engage:

> At the heart of our education and social problems in small indigenous cultures is the loss of cultural identity. Young people do not know who they are. Flowing from this lack of identity is a chain of consequences: low esteem . . . leading to feelings of disempowerment . . . leading to failure in school.[11]

At the start of my research in the high school, one teacher expressed enthusiasm for my project and its concerns with schooling, culture, race, and identity because, she pointed out, if we can help children to find and release their identity it will be a good thing. One reading of this teacher's claim might be that she sees identity as essential but suppressed and therefore capable of being released, as expressed in the UNESCO document. The fact that in both places, that is, in the South Pacific and here in the North American city of Toronto, cultural identity is understood as an entity that can be lost and, by extension, found speaks to the global authority of this particular discourse of culture.

According to this dominant view, subjects are the unified objects of a culture which tells us who we are. Cultures are viewed as objects that can be set against each other, so that "new cultures" and "not having a culture" are set against "old cultures" and "being at one with culture." Elusive culture, made from the fragments and mingling of representations, is a critique of this dominant discourse of culture. However, we must bear in mind that the sentiments expressed by both UNESCO and the Maple Heights teacher are frequently responses to the violence of racism and marginalization. Calling attention to the elusiveness of culture does not detract from the need to confront racist practices because culture must be used in antiracist actions. However we also need to note, as Michele Fine puts it, that "even 'for' Others there are growing stifling discourses that essentialize to make culture."[12] Indeed, to consider that culture is experienced ambivalently and in multiple and conflicting ways may well open new forms of antiracist practices that are capable of exceeding the old.

While the educational guide *Voices in a Seashell* offers us a rather narrow conceptualization of culture as a set of attributes, this view has until relatively recently been the dominant anthropological understanding of culture. More recently, though, in the field of anthropology (and in the humanities in general) this definition has become hotly contested—with the result, as James Clifford puts it, anthropology's culture is no longer what it used to be.[13]

In his elaboration of the culture concept, Raymond Williams notes that culture is an "exceptionally complex" term that, in English, initially described a process, as in the culture or cultivation of crops, rearing of animals, and tilling of the soil.[14] In the eighteenth and earlier part of the nineteenth century a "cultivated" person was one concerned with breeding practices, and was therefore viewed as possessing culture. Contemporary use of the word in the sense of "high culture" and "cultured persons" has its origins in this earlier notion of cultivation. Wagner suggests that anthropology helped to democratize this meaning by speaking of a "people's culture," thereby generalizing the idea of human refinement and domestication from individuals to collectives.[15] The shift in meaning is evident in late-nineteenth-century description of culture as "that complex whole" of beliefs, morals, customs, capabilities, and habits that people acquire as members of society.[16] This late-nineteenth-century articulation crystallized what I call *attribute theory*, the understanding of culture as a set of stable and knowable attributes. This theory dominated anthropological research and thinking for the greater part of the twentieth century. It underpinned the structural functionalist approach to the study of culture and an understanding of the concept as "coherent and predictable." It made it possible to talk about "patterns of culture" and to tie the concept to questions of nationalities.[17] In short, by the beginning of the twentieth century the meaning of culture had evolved into something quite different from its initial meaning in agriculture and horticulture.

The theory of culture as the attributes and distinguishing features of a community meant that ethnography, or writing culture, became the practice of recording and analyzing the traits that distinguished communities and groups. This approach, premised largely on modernist beliefs in objectivity and scientific models and a propensity for classification and ordering has subsequently been critiqued for objectifying and fixing cultural differences and for bringing to bear Western-centered assumptions upon the study of cultures considered non-Western.[18] Ironically, however, it is this attribute theory that was frequently borrowed in anthropology's second phase in the later part of the twentieth century to study ethnic and subcultures in Western multicultural settings.

If modernist beliefs in rationality, objectivity, and positivism shaped the theory and study of attribute culture, in the sixties and seventies concerns with subjectivity and the role of the anthropologist in "producing" culture marked a new phase in theorizing cultural phenomena.[19] Thus observes Roy Wagner, who called attention to how culture is "invented" in the process of being written about: "The study of culture is culture. . . . The study of culture is in fact our culture; it operates through our form, creates in our terms, borrows words and concepts for its meanings and re-creates us through our efforts."[20] To recall Toni Morrison, the subject of the dream is always the dreamer.[21]

One way for anthropologists to move beyond the previously unquestioned faith in objectivity and empiricism was to stress an interpretative approach, viewing culture as an open-ended text. Thinking about culture as text allows for multiple meanings and, as Geertz put it, insists upon the refinement of debates rather than the closure of consensus.[22] At the same time, anthropologists influenced by Marxism also urged us to think about how culture is not simply a naturally occurring phenomenon, but is situated within and shaped by systems of political economy.[23] The notion of elusive culture grows out of these earlier challenges to scientific models and their claims to being able to represent other cultures.

What might be identified as a third phase in the development of cultural theory emerged in the 1980s and is associated with what is called the "postmodernist turn."[24] In this third phase, debates on culture continue to critique ethnographic practices and authority. It is impossible to adequately survey the range of positions that mark this phase of critique except to note that among the influences are neo-Marxism, structuralism and poststructuralism, psychoanalytic theory, discourse theory, postmodernism, feminist theory, and postcolonial theory.[25] These various influences challenge the notion of the unitary, fixed subject, and insist upon the instability of meaning. They also open up questions about how the body is read and performed. Anthropological concerns with culture came to share with other academic disciplines a move away from grand theorizing and holistic explanations of "that complex whole" towards an interest in "partial truths." The monologic voice of the ethnographer gave way to an engagement with multiple voices that are competing and contradictory. Far from being a stable and knowable set of attributes, culture has now become a matter of debate about representations and the complex relationships that individuals take up in relation to them.

I have attempted to sketch out three phases as a crude periodization of developments in the theory of culture that have resulted in breaks in the ways that culture is theorized. Such an overview runs the risk of compromising the complex and dense field of cultural theory, and I ask the reader to keep this in mind. It is also important to keep in mind the relationships between these competing theories because such relations give rise to the lived tensions of identity and to the ways that culture is experienced. While new discourses, insights, and theories of culture may displace old theories, they do not replace them. Elusive culture must be understood in the light of competing and converging theories of culture. For example, and as will be seen in subsequent chapters, it takes account of the different forms of representations that are produced by attribute theory, but it also is attuned to the ambivalent and contradictory cultural processes of everyday lives.

Race

Perceptions of race as a natural and obvious given have long been challenged, not least by the discipline of anthropology. It is now commonplace to state that race is a social construct and a discursive category.[26] Thinking about race as discursive means understanding that races have been socially created and therefore have no intrinsic meaning outside their histories. While race might have a specific meaning in a given context and time, its significance changes in different circumstances and times. Studies of the construction of races demonstrate how the objectifying of racial difference coincided with and was contingent upon imperialism. Making racial categories was also in keeping with modernist obsessions with classification and ordering, a strategy for control. When different races were attached to different cultures and regions of the world, discourses of race also became discourses of geography and culture.[27] It is the crosscutting and mapping of different discourses onto bodies that make race a discursive category, but at the same time one of the most naturalized discourses available for making sense of the world.[28]

Being a discursive category means that the signs and meanings that are subsumed by race can be quite broad and subject to change. This was aptly illustrated when I asked a group of university students to make a random list of the everyday key words that are evoked by the concept *race*. The list was wide ranging and included the following: peoples' looks, skin color, culture, religion, musical tastes, hairstyles, place of birth, dress, intelligence, attitudes, identity, beliefs, and history. This spontaneous list demonstrates that when it comes to thinking about race, it is difficult to pin down stable and singular meanings or to distinguish materiality from interpretation. In its everyday operations, race draws upon and draws together a variety of discourses affixed to human bodies. This observation also shows how the theoretical distinctions between *ethnicity* as about culture and *race* as about biology fall down in everyday practice. In the chapters that follow, we will see that through these discursive practices, race can be many things.

Various genealogies of race suggest that its attachment to biology is relatively new.[29] The present day practice of replacing biological explanations for race with cultural ones might well signal a return to older, more rigid forms of classification.[30] In recent years we have witnessed a resurgence of interest in race sciences even as beliefs in racial hierarchies have long been discredited. "New racism" is a term that was coined to describe the shift from crude forms of scientific racism based on biologically determined social hierarchy to racism premised on belief in immutable cultural differences. This newer form of racism may be couched in a language of "values," "incompatible cultures," and "complex differences," effectively discriminating without even using the word "race." New racism also draws upon discourses of nation in order to suggest belonging or not-belonging, inclusion and exclusion. For example, when a columnist writing in one of Canada's respected magazines poses the question, "Why have Black activists trotted out this tired old rhetoric about systemic racism?" and answers her own question by stating, "Canadians know themselves and they know that Canadian society is not racist," the identity "Black activist" is thereby constituted as incompatible with "Canadian."[31] A similar practice is at play when Ontario's premier attempts to dismiss a demonstration against his government's social and economic policies on the grounds that he saw Iranians and Iraqis taking part in the march. Race, articulated through the codes of nation, culture, and identity, divides those who belong from those who are made other.

One of the symptoms of these new forms of racism is the presentation of observation as fact, as in the instances cited above. This practice produces the sense of an objective discourse that is outside the speaker's opinions and evaluations—one is only describing what one sees. But discourse analysis requires us to think about the situation of what one sees, and the power of specific locations and institutional bases. Such an analysis interprets discourse as a site of struggle where groups strive and compete for the production of meaning and for authoritative expertise. In the next chapter the concept new racism becomes significant for understanding the subtle ways by which such struggles are waged at the site of schooling. We will also see that new racism is further complicated by discourses of multiculturalism and immigration and claims about declining standards. In the same way that the meaning of culture changes, so shall we see that the meanings attached to race by students at Maple Heights also shift and change.

Identity

Much of the growing field of literature on the question of identity is structured by tension between conceptualizations of identity as a category or as a process. As a category, identity announces who we are and calls upon notions of nation, class, gender, and ethnicity for definition. But a second way of talking about identities recognizes that identity is a process of making identifications, a process that is continuous and incomplete. This distinction between identity and identification is important because while the former implies an essential and fixed individual, the latter recognizes that identity is a constructed and open-ended process. The concept of identification raises critical questions about the complex relationships that youth form in a context of multiplying lifestyle possibilities, and enables the researcher to observe the kinds of identifications that youth are making. The researcher can note how these might shift and change in contradictory ways, rather than search for the authoritative youth culture and identity.

With respect to questions of human subjectivity, Hall distinguishes three concepts of identity linked to three overlapping models of how the subject is conceptualized. They are the Enlightenment subject, the sociological subject, and the postmodern subject.[32] The Enlightenment subject has an innate inner core which unfolds as the individual moves through life. Identity, within this framework, is the linear development and unfolding of the individual's essential core or self. The sociological subject is the product of the increasing complexity of modernity. What the Enlightenment saw as an autonomous inner core, sociological models view as being mediated and produced by cultures and socialization. In social psychological terms, identity, and the self, is the result of symbolic interaction between the individual and what Mead and others term "significant others."[33] Identity offers coherence and completion to relationships between the subject and the social world. But this sense of unity, security, and coherence is, Hall points out, a fantasy in a world where identities multiply, fragment, become contradictory, and remain unresolved.[34] It is this latter condition of fragmentation, of multiple, competing identities, that makes for the postmodern subject. Within this category, subjects are no longer perceived as fastened to cultures and external social structures. It is important to note, however, that this third notion of the subject does not mean that identity cannot produce feelings of security, rootedness, and coherence. Instead it recognizes that such feelings arise from the practice of constructing and situating the self within narratives. This means, Hall reminds us, that identity exists in relation to representations that anchor the subject in the social world.[35]

While youth experiment and play in the making of race, and while their cultural practices might be quite elusive, they may at the same time be acted upon by racist stereotypes that adhere to race as stable and predictable. Such tensions are central to the question of making identity. I do not use "tension" to suggest a condition that can and should be resolved, but rather as central to the ways that identity is theorized. There are not only tensions between lived experiences and outside prejudices, but also within subjects, between similitude and difference. When we declare who we are, the markers that we might borrow often seem both sufficient and inadequate, perhaps because the categories to which we appeal do not offer any guarantee of stability or social recognition, nor do they fulfill the desire for recognition that may precede the ways we name ourselves. These shortcomings of naming identity are an important theme in the chapters that follow. This ethnography of Maple Heights stresses the question of identity as a process of making identifications—identifications made, for example, with the different cultural and racialized representations and the multiplying lifestyle possibilities that mark the arena within which social relations are forged. But as we shall see, the kinds of identifications that are made by the subjects in this study, mainly youth at Maple Heights, are never complete. They are always in process and are therefore partial and often contradictory.

Globalization, Diaspora, and Difference

I want to draw attention to three larger dynamics that open new challenges and have forced the need to re-examine the questions of culture, race, and identity in relation to schooling. These are globalization, diaspora, and difference, respectively. Again I ask the reader to keep in mind the relationships among these dynamics.

Globalization

Although the concept "globalization" came into use to refer to the specific conditions that distinguish the closing decade of the twentieth century, these conditions go back several hundred years. Globalization signals the internationalization of capitalism and the rapid circulation and flow of information, commodities, and visual images around the world. The technological developments associated with these times have changed the nature of global and local relations and challenged many of the binaries that were taken for granted, such as insider and outsider, and the "West and the rest."[36] Processes of globalization have significantly changed perceptions of time and space and rendered problematic notions of identity as fixed in time and space.[37] These late-twentieth-century developments have also challenged belief in culture as tied to place. The developments of globalization ask us instead to pay attention to "cultural flows," "creolization," and the "deterritorialization" of culture.[38] In short, the dynamics to which globalization refers have changed the nature of the arena in which questions of identity, culture, and race are now being posed. These dynamics are also contradictory because while globalization erodes national identities, these and other identities are also being strengthened as resistance to globalization. Further-more, while national identities as they have been traditionally known are in decline, new identities of hybridity are taking their place.[39]

In the chapters that follow we will see that while the youth in the Toronto high school identify closely with a specific part of the city, they are at the same time partners in cultures that circulate globally. The local, namely the school and the location wherein they live, is at the intersection of the global. Under these conditions, the media and now the Internet have come to profoundly influence how individuals see their place in the world. Social space is constructed out of social processes that occur elsewhere, so that as Massey suggests, the place to which we belong might best be thought of as a part and moment in the global network of social relations and understandings.[40] Under these conditions, associations with multiple places and transnational identities are commonplace, and individuals in Toronto may well feel closer to family and friends in Latin America, Africa, Asia, or Europe than they do to the neighbors in the apartment above or those next door. The question of loyalty and belonging to the nation-state, in this case Canada, may appear to be at stake under these new conditions, as we shall see in chapter 2. But perhaps what is really at stake is the question of how the nation is imagined and the possibilities that these late-twentieth- and early-twenty-first-century conditions open up for new kinds of imagining.

Diaspora

In its original use, "diaspora" referred to the dispersal of a people from a homeland and the multiple journeys that form collective memories and the desire for return to the place of origin, imaginary or real. However, diaspora has also come to refer to the conditions of living with multiplace associations and of being immersed in social networks that span different countries. It is a concept that has associations with human displacement and today encompasses both forced and voluntary migrations. Unlike its original use, in much contemporary theorizing diaspora is used to critique the claims that fixed origins and identities are dependent on a center to which one hopes to return. Contemporary understanding of diasporic means being at home in the place where one lives while still living with the memories and shared histories of the place from which one or one's ancestors have come. Living with a diasporic identity might well mean that the relationship to the imaginary homeland is an ambivalent one. Discourses of "roots" may invoke nostalgia, but "home" remains a place of no return. For many of the youth in this study, Toronto is the place to which they belong, though belonging may also be about relationships with other places.

Avtar Brah makes the useful distinction between diaspora and "diaspora space." While the former describes everyday life experiences built in relation to stories of movement and displacement, diaspora space is where diasporic peoples converge and where multiple subject positions and identities are proclaimed, juxtaposed, contested, and disavowed. It is the place where the permitted and the prohibited are perpetually interrogated:

> Diaspora space is the point at which boundaries of inclusion and exclusion, of belonging and otherness, of "us" and "them" are contested. . . . It includes the entanglement, the intertwining of the genealogies of dispersion with those of "staying put." The diaspora space is the site where the native is as much a diasporian as the diasporian is a native.[41]

The notion of a diaspora space is useful for understanding how the school is the stage for the enactment of native Canadian and diasporan identities—a place of contests between belonging and otherness, and the making and remaking of nation.

Diaspora thus refers to the historical experience of movement and dispersal of peoples, but we may also draw on diaspora as a theoretical concept that helps us to think about culture and cultural processes as forged through transnational networks and identifications. Such an understanding of diaspora and its relationship to culture, identity, and race is important if we are to understand the complex processes of making identities and cultures among Toronto high school students, the majority of whom were born elsewhere.

Difference

This third concept, "difference," is frequently related to discourses of globalization and diaspora. It is usually talked about in terms of the social attributes of different cultures, but it is also used as a critique of the essentialism and assumptions about fixity made by this first understanding of the word. Difference in the first sense is used to refer to separate cultures, communities, and social formations and to distinguish between groups. This notion of difference is what is often invoked by multiculturalist discourses that talk about "different cultures." The problem with this meaning of difference is that it relies upon the principle of a common denominator, or what Toni Morrison calls an "economy of stereotypes," in order to recognize different cultures.[42]

In the second sense the word is used to grapple with difference within groups. It refers to experiences of change, transformation, and hybridity. As Rutherford puts it, this difference asserts identities as unfixed and critiques the ways identities may be "overdetermined" by reference to cultures.[43] Thus while identity might invoke notions of sameness, asserting difference stresses discontinuity within sameness.[44] Within this second understanding of difference individuals may mimic the cultural attributes through which they are defined, but they assert their individual differences by mocking and displacing those same attributes. This notion of difference is particularly significant in this study of youth at Maple Heights.

The concept difference may therefore complicate discourses of culture because while it is frequently invoked to imply commonality, as in individuals sharing a common culture that is different from another, it also refers to disruptions, discontinuities, or difference within the shared culture. Difference is about the similitude attached to different cultures. But difference as used in this work is about undermining the assumptions upon which beliefs in similitude are premised. Difference in this sense borrows from Rutherford, who sees it as "an experience of change, transformation and hybridity" and "a critique of essentialism and mono-culturalism."[45]

Multiculturalism and Antiracism

This ethnography of identity, race, and youth in a Toronto high school is also in conversation with two large and growing fields of research in education, multiculturalism and antiracism. I will point to some of the significant trends in the volume of research on multiculturalism, antiracism, and inclusive education that are especially relevant to the focus on Maple Heights.

In Canada ethnocentric policies of assimilation into an imagined dominant culture went unquestioned for the greater part of the twentieth century. An extreme example of the resulting racism was the forced removal of Native American children from their homes and families in order to "exorcize" them of their "malignant" culture.[46] Such policies, however, were undermined in the latter part of the sixties and the early seventies. The challenges came from a number of directions including decolonization movements, theories of liberation, increasing concerns with human rights and cultural difference, and, of particular significance, the influence of the civil rights movement in the United States. The challenges that came from these various directions coincided with massive demographic changes throughout the world. Demographic changes in the 1970s were such that in Toronto, now recognized as a global city, it was estimated that there were as many as seventy different ethnic groups or subgroups, and about four hundred ethnic organizations contending for place.[47]

In the early seventies the Federal Government of Canada took measures to replace the policies of assimilation with support for cultural pluralism, and in 1971 it declared multiculturalism an official state policy. This policy was based on a view of Canada as a "cultural mosaic," suggestive of a wide range of ethnic cultures coexisting as the nation.[48] This view of Canada sought to distinguish itself from the "melting pot" of the United States. In the field of education, in Canada as in countries like the United States, Britain, and Australia, cultural pluralism and multiculturalism are premised on the belief that learning about one's own culture, heritage, or ethnic roots will boost self-esteem, improve the performance of minority students, and reduce prejudice toward groups that are different from one's own. However, framed by a "folk model" discourse of culture, and disarticulated from social and economic inequalities, multiculturalism may celebrate cultural differences while at the same time perpetuating racist practices and beliefs. It was this realization that gave rise to the more proactive policies of antiracism.

Subsequent theories and policies of antiracism in Canada followed upon the British critiques that argued that while multiculturalism privileged "lifestyles," antiracism was more interested in "life chances" and in addressing the structural inequalities and the impact that racism has on the schooling of minority students.[49] This was an important strategic distinction as it called attention to the different ways that racism operates within the school system and institutions in general. However, despite marking distinctions, multiculturalism and antiracism still share a view of culture as a set of knowable attributes and value the mutual coexistence of cultures as discrete and bounded entities.[50] As Paul Gilroy notes, the emphasis on race as culture, identity, and ethnic essence rather than as politics and history is congruent with the nationalist concerns of both the political right and the antiracist left. This left includes many within the Black community who develop their own fascination with ethnic difference, and in the process reduce political definitions of race to a narcissistic celebration of culture and identity.[51]

Both multiculturalism and antiracism assume, as Friedman expresses it, that just as we have a gene pool, so too do we have a culture pool.[52] Challenging the gene pool analogy, elusive culture is interested in the more ambivalent processes of making culture and the often troubled relationship between cultural and personal identity. While elusive culture recognizes, with Cohen, the need for "reductive representations" of racism in order to achieve specific political goals, at the same time it critiques the practice of disavowing complexity for the sake of political ideals and moral certainties.[53] "Elusive culture" exceeds a view of subjects as simply objects of culture or of identity categories as being definitive of cultures by considering the tensions, contradictions, and surprises in the ways youths make culture and identities.

Doing the Ethnography

"Fieldwork" is the term anthropologists use to describe their extended periods of participant observation and interviewing "in the field." In anthropology's earlier days anthropologists traveled to a distant place, "lived among the natives," learned their language, and spent long periods of time recording and translating their culture to make it intelligible to an audience. This practice of ethnography was, in large part, the means by which the West came to know its Other and, paradoxically, to know itself. As noted, such a view of culture, ethnographic authority, and the detached observer has long been considered problematic.[54] Postcolonial theorists interrogate the binaries of West and Other;[55] globalization challenges belief in culture as a bounded entity tied to place;[56] and postmodern theorizing asks us to consider the poetics of writing, the significance of representations, and the ways by which the participants, authors, and readers are all implicated in the production and reception of the text.[57] These developments are such that ethnography might also become, as expressed by Britzman, "a contested and fictive geography" because the identities of those involved, "including author and reader—are, in essence, textualized identities, a cacophony and dialogic display of contradictory desires, fears and literary tropes, that, if carefully 'read' suggest just how slippery speaking, writing, and reading subjectively really is."[58]

At Maple Heights the school day begins at 8:50 A.M. when students stand in their classrooms to the Canadian national anthem played over a public address system. The anthem is followed by a very short reading, sometimes little more than one sentence, which is billed as the "thought for the day." Quite early in my year at Maple Heights the reading was a sentence by Canadian novelist Margaret Atwood. It was a simple and perhaps self-evident statement: "The answers we get in literature depend on the questions we ask." Simple as it was, the thought prompted me to think, "For 'literature' read 'anthropology and the social sciences in general.'" As I took my place among a class of older and more advanced students to listen to their presentations on a range of issues including domestic violence, youth and crime, and the issue of zero tolerance,[59] the Atwood reading gave me the opportunity for timely reflection on methodology and the age-old questions of objectivity and subjectivity in doing research.

While recognizing their limits, in undertaking this

research I utilized the classic anthropological methods of participant observation and extensive interviewing. I spent an average of four days per week for a full academic year at Maple Heights. There are two main advantages of spending extended periods in one place. first, an extended observation means witnessing the shifts and changes that occur over time and the contradictions and tensions that might mark identity as contextual and historical. Second, time is a necessary factor for building confidence and trust. I undertook participant observation in a wide range of settings including classrooms, the library, hallways, the cafeteria, the drama studio, the art studio, the music room and, when the weather made it possible, in the parking lot and on the playing fields. I also spent time during lunch periods with students in the nearby shopping mall. My interviews were one-on-one as well as group conversations, and both formal, in the sense of a set time and place, and informal, in the sense of spontaneous extended conversations around the school.

I was given the opportunity to both facilitate and take part in discussions on a variety of subjects linked to my research with students in English classes. Discussions with grade nine classes, for example, offered interesting insights into the wide range of backgrounds and places of origin represented at Maple Heights. Discussions and writing exercises with grade ten and eleven students resulted in written works on culture and identities, an example of which I draw upon at the end of this chapter. Work with grade twelve and Ontario Advanced Certificate (OAC) students did not result in written work, but the class discussions were useful for offering insight into the various musical tastes and youth cultural trends that are represented at Maple Heights. Other approaches to research were experimental. For example, with grade eleven classes I facilitated a media project, the aim of which was to produce twenty-minute videos of different aspects of life at the school. Also of special importance was a drama project with grade eleven students which resulted in three half-hour videos on identity. Participants performed monologues on personal identity and worked on sketches in which they explored different themes and sites around which identity is contested, such as family, peer groups, ethnicity, and racism. Close involvement in these sorts of projects provided possibilities for working with students and building the appropriate networks while being able to collect data.

Tape recordings were made of some of the formal or pre-arranged conversations. In other cases, handwritten notes were made and written up at the end of the day. In all I recorded forty interviews with students drawn from grades ten, eleven, twelve, and OAC, and made notes on an additional thirty. Instead of recorded interviews with grade nine students, I held class discussions. In addition, I had conversations with twenty-five of the forty teachers and staff, of which only four were recorded. While these various conversations are the main source of data for this ethnography, I make no attempt to represent them as realist ethnography. The aim instead is to reflect upon the various fragments of discourse from which these conversations draw and to call attention to the possible relationships and associations that might be made among these various fragments. I also attempt to draw attention to the cooperative and collaborative nature of this ethnographic project.[60] In writing this account I draw upon the postmodern concepts of reflexivity, collage, montage, and dialogism.[61]

I have noted the multiple approaches that I adopted for this ethnography, including having students talk and write about identity. Striking about some of this work were the ways students themselves theorize identity and their challenges to the tendencies to fix and essentialize identity, race, and culture in multicultural and antiracist discourses. They also stress the social and relational importance of identity. Identity was thus variously described in short pieces of writing by students as "the way you want to be perceived," "the way you are recognized by others," or "things you do for people to see you." Most students recognized that identity is a process. As one stated, "Your identity is developed gradually over years." They were aware of the importance of youth: "Youth is the period which determines what your identity will be when you are older." Another student remarked, "I believe that a person's identity is created and molded depending on how easily that person can be influenced by others." Others noted the importance of consumption and style in making identity: "Identity is made up of the clothes you wear, what music you listen to, or even small things such as how you do your hair. It could mean a lot of things, however it is mostly the small individual things that makes a person unique."

In these various observations and theories students appear to depart from the discourses that fix culture and identity. Also significant was the realization of the difficulties in talking and writing about identity: "In your mind you know exactly who you are and how you want to be perceived but if someone wants you to explain or discuss your identity your mind goes immediately blank and you are left speechless." Such observations recognize that identities are always partial. When one explains who or what one is, the description can never satisfy the desire to be recognized as a complex subject. This is a necessary inadequacy of identity. It is a shortcoming in any talk of identity because, as the same student points out, "identities change everyday, sometimes for the better, sometimes for the worse. But in the end it is all up to us to try to be the person we want to be."

Another writing exercise undertaken by grade twelve students used metaphors for thinking about the complexity of identity. In this exercise, identity was collapsed with personality. It was poetically compared to "sponges in the pool of life, absorbing knowledge and understanding in order to develop their identity." Other metaphors included the Shame-o-lady flower, "bright and blooming when no one is looking but the minute some one sees me or touches it, it gets shy and goes into hiding, closes up." There was a "jigsaw puzzle" that requires "time and patience to be fully understood," and a "coconut" that makes it difficult to see "the real me on the inside" because of "the hard barrier protecting the self from getting hurt." finally there was the metaphor of the river, deceptive since one is unable to tell how deep it is just by looking at it, what the mouth would be like, or whether it is smooth or rough.

Many of the themes that emerge in this snapshot of how youth at Maple Heights theorize identity we will see recurring throughout this ethnography. This initial glimpse, however, demonstrates how the academic distinctions that are made among such factors as race, nation, identity, and culture all become unfastened and muddled in the discourse of youth. At first this observation might seem insignificant, but it is quite crucial because it opposes the discourses and the structures, the procedures and the orientations, of much of what goes on under the names of multiculturalism and antiracism. We see here, and will see more clearly as this ethnography proceeds, that the students do not discuss their desires and worries, their views and aspirations by settling upon a definition of identity, culture, or race once and for all. Furthermore, as the processes of globalization might suggest, identity unfolds as an odd combination of first- and second-hand memories, shifting geographies, desire for community, and resistance to being contained by community all at the same time. These are the complications and tensions of the everyday ways by which identity is lived.

Overview of Chapters

The complications and tensions of culture, race, and identity are a consistent theme in the chapters that follow. In chapter 2, I constitute Maple Heights High School as a discursive space, and move away from constructions of ethno-graphic sites as devoid of the subjectivities of those who populate them. I draw largely upon conversations with teachers at Maple Heights that took place over the year that I spent in the school and show how in this space of school-ing discourses of identity, history, nationhood, and multi-culturalism are conflated, crosscut, and mapped onto one another. The three subsequent chapters work more closely with student conversations, and I ask the reader to note the relationships between these two levels of discourse—that of the students and that of their teachers.

Chapter 3 describes conversations I had with students who were part of a school program called Positive Peer Culture. I use the metaphor "portraits" to think about the construction of identities in this chapter, and show how students make (and resist making) identifications in rela-tion to one another, peer groups, diaspora, and commu-nity.

In chapter 4 I draw largely on one-on-one conversations to focus on race. I draw attention to the complex and con-tradictory ways race is imagined and lived. In this chapter the impossibility of separating race, culture, and identity is evi-dent, and discourses of race are muddled with discourses of nation and community.

Chapter 5 centers on a public discussion of interracial dating organized by a group of students calling themselves "The African Queens." The chapter examines race as a set of social relations and also draws attention to how a politics of identity may shape the workings of race in public spaces. By inserting accounts of the public meeting between discus-sions of private conversations, I call attention to how what one argues for in public might be set in tension with what one thinks and does in private. I give special attention to conflations of race and gender, how race becomes gendered, and how gender becomes racialized. But I also call attention to how gendered and racialized subjectivities are made through secrets, fantasies, and conflicting desires as well as through the range of racial stereotypes that abound.

In the final chapter I return to the dilemma of writing elusive culture and the ethnographer's implication in fixing in representation what we observe as fluid. While I underscore the importance of understanding the cultures of youth and the culture of schooling as emergent rather than foreclosed, I stress that elusive culture does not emerge in a vacuum. I therefore ask readers to keep in mind the relations of power and the sets of tensions wherein and from which culture emerges. Indeed the book calls attention to a whole set of tensions that mark the making of race, culture, and identity. These include tensions between the various cultural representations and the different identity categories that are available on the one hand, and the complex subject positions that are taken up by individuals on the other; tensions between the desire for continuity in the notion of "roots" and how they are continually reworked through "routes"; and tensions between rigid ways of thinking about knowledge and identity and the fluid and multiple affiliations that youth make in their everyday practices. With respect to the question of schooling, this book ultimately raises the question of what it might mean to conceive of these sets of tensions as opportunities rather than impediments to learning and pedagogic practices.

2

The Discursive Space
of Schooling

To visit Maple Heights is a bit like going to the United Nations, that is, if you think of the UN as a place where different-looking peoples from around the globe meet. In this sense Maple Heights can be seen as reflective of Greater Toronto, which has been designated "the most ethnically diverse city in the world." I did have some knowledge of the diversity of Maple Heights when possibilities were being explored for undertaking research in the school.

Maple Heights was recommended as a place that might be open to my research project if I could show that it would be useful to educators thinking about questions of diversity and schooling in these global times. Subsequently, my proposal for exploring the question of identity was met by the school principal with optimism and enthusiasm. There was also caution. The unspoken message was that Maple Heights would not welcome research that was simply about "fishing for racists." However, it seemed that the principal and I were interested in the same kinds of questions. As our conversation continued, she explained that the vital challenge facing the school was to build "what was traditionally called

'school spirit'" in these times of multiculturalism and competing claims to inclusive education.[1] We agreed on the
importance of building communities premised on, rather
than suppressing, multiple differences. One of Maple
Heights' teachers, in a different conversation, described the
challenge as finding ways to "make the mix work."

What this exploratory conversation suggested to me was
that Maple Heights was grappling with change, a struggle
that confronted entrenched models of what the school used
to be. Over the subsequent weeks school personnel
described their sense of the changes, often in terms of an
imaginary coherent school identity now fragmenting under
the impact of cultural pluralism and competing interests. At
the time of this research, the question of the school's identity and the competing identities of its students was further
complicated by concerns with school and street violence and
their representation in the media, so that building school
spirit was also articulated as creating a safe climate where
students could be "proud to be able to say that they come to
this school."[2]

The guarded optimism for my work on the part of the
principal was shared by other administrators and teachers at
Maple Heights, but it was by no means universal. There were
also instances, particularly in the early days, of resistance and
suspicion from some staff. But like good modes of resistance, this was caged in a language of wanting to ensure that
the study would be representative and objective. For example, following the presentation of my research project to the
school staff, one of the teachers met me in the parking lot
and wanted to know why Maple Heights was being used for
my study. Why not look at different schools? What is the
information going to be used for? What is the agenda? How
was I going to address the differences that exist among the
various schools that fall under the jurisdiction of this
school's board of education? But interesting things can also
happen in long-term ethnographic fieldwork—the teacher

who at first seemed most resistant became, in the language of fieldwork, one of my key informants. This teacher and others allowed me to observe the more complex and often contradictory ways by which teachers imagine the past, and observe and theorize their present. In the process they may simultaneously resist, accommodate, and be ambivalent toward the discourses of multiculturalism, antiracism, and inclusivity all at the same time. In such cases, Bhabha reminds us, one attitude may take account of reality while the other may be under influences that detach the ego from reality.[3] Put another way, these are instances that illustrate how subjects might be pulled in one direction by the authoritative discourses on multiculturalism and inclusivity, and pushed in the opposite direction by internally persuasive discourses and their conflicting desires and interests.[4] The tensions within subjects may be similar to those that shape relations between subjects. For example, at Maple Heights teachers who appeared to be actively committed to exploring what they imagined multicultural and antiracist policies expected of them might be criticized and caricatured as "politically correct" or "caught up in their own mission" by those who were indifferent or opposed to what they believed these policies required of them. In these ways competing discourses shaped relations among teachers as they also produced tensions within individual teachers.

In the rest of this chapter, I map out Maple Heights as a discursive field wherein identities are made, unmade, and contested. As "data" I draw on my conversations with twenty-five teachers whose time spent teaching at Maple Heights ranged from thirty years in one case to less than one academic year in another. I place "data" in quotation marks in order to stress the dialogic dimension of doing this "fieldwork" and to emphasize the cooperative and collaborative nature of this ethnographic situation.[5] Recognizing that data is mutually produced by ethnographer and subjects contrasts with the modernist belief that the observer and observed are unencumbered by each other.[6] The school, I argue, is not simply a container of identities or a static locale, but is implicated in the production of the identities of teachers and students. Conversely, the making of the identities of its teachers and students is also the making of the school's identity. Researching schooling as a discursive space consequently means juxtaposing the various fragments of discourses to consider how these act upon the actor's views of what is going on.[7] This approach to research does not mean that the facts and figures traditionally used in ethnographies to give a realist picture of the ethnographic site are not important. More important for what follows, however, is how the past, present, and future are imagined and what discourses and associations are summoned in these imaginings. While I occasionally draw on accounts and images inscribed in the school's yearbooks, I pull most from conversations because it is in the social memories and the representations that are invoked by these conversations that the perceptions and anxieties of the present are read.

History, Location, and Class

Maple Heights is located in an area that one of the teachers, himself a demographer, described as being among the poorest in metropolitan Toronto. The economic recession in effect at the time of this research, it was claimed, had a particularly bad effect on the area. But the socioeconomic status that is attached to the school, and to those who attend it, is not clearly discernable from the school's immediate vicinity. Semidetached and detached homes with neatly trimmed lawns facing the school on one side, and the sense of space and openness on another, are not normally associated with poverty or the inner city. One teacher who was born and raised in this area and attended Maple Heights in its earlier days pointed out that at one stage this area would have been somewhat middle class but was now working class because of the rising standards of what it means to be "middle." The immediate area is also described as an "ageing area" as children of earlier immigrants move out—a sign of upward social mobility—leaving behind grandparents. Such demographic shifts are one of the causes of growing concern with Maple Height's declining enrollment. The population density of the surrounding area is relatively low. The majority of students at the school, however, come not from these surrounding homes but from high-rise apartment blocks some ten minutes by bus to the west of the school. Some of these apartments are government-assisted accommodations.

Though quite removed from the actual center of metropolitan Toronto, Maple Heights is reconstituted in discourse as an "inner-city" school. The discourse of inner city, as we will see below, collapses concerns with race, welfare, crime, and even violence. One teacher, who identified as middle class and was at the beginning of her teaching career, described her earlier impressions of the school and its location: "It's branded a high-immigrant area with associations with welfare, crime, and just not the same kind of education." But this reputation, she was quick to point out, is quite unfounded because "it is not like that at all and there are so many really nice students here." She also claimed that the negative associations produce a sense of cohesiveness, mutual dependence, and community because of "a pervasive feeling of being threatened." However, another teacher claimed that the same discourse that criminalizes the school and its geographical community produces divisions, a lack of motivation, and a lack of community. Here, while the discourses are described through comparable lenses, their effects are theorized differently.

Maple Heights Secondary School was founded as Maple Heights Collegiate in 1955. Its founding coincided with large-scale postwar immigration to Canada, and to the city of Toronto in particular, from Europe. Maple Heights' vicinity, like many regions of Toronto, has been a reception area for recent immigrants, as has the school itself. The school's history and identity are consequently constructed in relation to the various waves of immigration to the area. Events within the school cannot be separated from what happens demographically around it. However, the details of this history are contested by those who relate them.

In the early days of its history, Maple Heights Collegiate established a reputation for high academic standards.[8] By definition, a collegiate is a high school that focuses more on academics than on the traditional trades. In these earlier times, when the school population was three times its present size, which meant having about fifteen hundred students, one teacher claimed that school spirit used to be "more vibrant and much more academic" and cited photographs of grand musicals in the school yearbook as support for this claim. He imagined these earlier times as being ethnically and racially homogeneous. While a different teacher also claimed that there was a very strong Jewish presence at Maple Heights in its earlier years, he stressed that the school was never homogeneous in this sense. Ethnicity, race, and talk of standards were frequently intertwined in these conversations, as in the following comment from a teacher: "This school used to have some very academic people. It was a strong Jewish community. And so you had this work ethic thing." Such relationships between the concepts *academic people, Jewish community,* and *work ethic,* effectively racialize work ethics and standards and disparage the present diverse population. Such a view of the past, however, was challenged by yet another teacher who had also taught in the school for more than twenty years, and who claimed that "there was always a strong Anglo-Saxon element," and cautioned against images of a glorious Jewish past.

The imagined Jewish dominance at Maple Heights gave way to a new ethnic group in the late sixties and early seventies as increasing numbers of Italian immigrants came to settle in the area and attend the school. The Jewish presence diminished with this new wave of immigration as more and more people from that community moved away from the immediate vicinity of Maple Heights and to the east of the city. This development some teachers noted as a sign of upward mobility, but one claimed that such a pattern is also illustrative of "immigrants attracting their own kind." The teacher who had noted the strong Anglo-Saxon presence also mentioned that these new immigrants were "highly motivated" but that there was always talk of things declining as different groups came into the vicinity and the school. He went on to describe how northern Italian students expressed their concerns and warnings about the problems to be expected from the increasing numbers of southern Italians coming to live in the city.

By 1975, the narrative continues, the Italians lost their demographic dominance, as ethnic groups including an identifiable Black group and Korean- and Spanish-speaking immigrants moved to the neighborhood. By the end of the seventies the shift from predominantly Jewish to mostly Italian gave way to "the fifty-seven varieties," a reference to the presence of students and their parents who came not just from Europe, but from Latin American, the Caribbean, Africa, Asia, and the Indian Subcontinent. In the late seventies, Vietnamese students, known as "the boat people," began to arrive. One teacher claimed that many of these refugees were "superb" in terms of attitudes toward school, "but then, they were largely from families that had money and this shows the importance of socioeconomic factors." In the late seventies and early eighties there were also large building projects to the west of the school. Of these developments one teacher suggested that "the building of high-rise government housing in the area, together with the fact that students had to go to school in order for parents to qualify for welfare, meant a major change in the socioeconomic makeup of the school."

I have noted how in the telling of Maple Heights' history, a discourse of immigration often draws upon the subtexts of welfare and, in some instances, even crime. This is how the "third wave," which in the imagination of one informant produced an exodus of Italians from the area, is described: "The vacuum created by the exodus of the Italians from this area was then filled with refugees and immigrants. The new immigrants were from the West Indies, Asia, and then you had the boat people." A second teacher drew on the populist discourse which constitutes immigrants as "visible" by describing the school population as changing "from ninety percent Italian to ninety percent immigrant." In the telling of the history we see Italians lose their visibility and become nonimmigrant. Lost in the same moment is a specific history of discrimination against this particular group of immigrants from southern Europe.

It was in the seventies that the school's status changed from collegiate to secondary school. Officially this new designation meant that a variety of workshops were set up to offer practically based courses to complement the existing academic program. This was a time, teachers believed, when extracurricular clubs flourished in the school. However, this nostalgia is contested. Although one teacher lamented that today's youth are different and that Maple Heights no longer had "the same kinds of students," another was quick to point out that with a student population of just under five hundred, the school is one-third the size that it was in the seventies. At the end-of-year special awards assembly that I attended, it was clear that there were still many activities taking place at Maple Heights. Those of us present for the ceremony were amazed by the range of activities that had taken place during the course of that academic year.

For teachers, juxtaposing memories with perceptions of the present is a contradictory process. The present, for example, was critiqued by one teacher as a time when youth are "into mainstream cool" and "more interested in image and identity" or in "joining the ranks for self-esteem." It was then recalled that in the early seventies, "Italians were already beginning to work after school and the kids were getting into cars and clothes" because "parents were also wanting to provide these things for them because of the idea of their children having it better than they did."

In these discursive constructions of Maple Heights, teachers' descriptions of how things were and subsequently have become were enmeshed in various discourses of resentment, popular conservatism, and new racism. In the claims and counterclaims about the past and the present, multiculturalism and antiracism were sometimes invoked as disadvantaging "us" (meaning White Canadians). However, this sometimes occurred in ways that posited themselves as for rather than against multicultural and antiracist sentiments. For example, it was suggested that Black students were now unfairly receiving all the attention, and this observation was made as a statement of solidarity with the other minorities who were being sidelined. Similarly it was suggested that "now the White students are feeling as though they are the minority." But the same teacher qualified this position, saying, "Actually together each group is now feeling excluded." Another strategy for negotiating and reworking these discourses is to pose questions: Why have African History Month? Why not have an Italian History Month? Why not set aside each month to deal with the different regions of the world? Such questions are posited not as critiques of present policies, but as mere suggestions as to how they could be made even better. In this way, opposing positions and strategies of resistance may be concealed under a banner of fairness and reason.

These claims about identity and culture are all framed by the trope of cultural relativism that sees cultures as discrete, bounded, and contending for positions on the multicultural Canadian stage, and within the school in particular. This conjures up notions of a battle for multiculturalism in which there are winners and losers, victims and victimizers. But positions in the contest are changeable. While one can be sympathetic about all the cultures that are being neglected and left out, one can also state that "now we feel like the underdog. We have to be submissive to others; otherwise we are seen as racists." Another position alleges that "you're damned if you do and damned if you don't" and that "foreigners are now telling us that we are stupid for letting things go this far." The self, reconstituted here as Canada, has a continuity and coherence that is disrupted by cultural difference, read onto the students who embody the different cultures at Maple Heights. The "multicultural wars" are in this way another aspect of Bauman's "war on ambivalence,"[9] in this instance quietly waged in the interest of securing a stable meaning of "Canadian." In the discursive space of Maple Heights questions of nation underpin questions of school identity, multiculturalism, and antiracism, and the school is reconstituted as a microcosm of the nation at large. As such there are those who are read as belonging, those who are made "other," and those who are somewhere in between.

The question of how the nation is imagined and what constitutes a Canadian identity, as if there can only be one, is perpetually posed in Canada. In an October 1995 article in the *Toronto Star*, Tom Walkom presented a popular representation of what makes Canada "Canada." At a time when Quebec's distinct identity and the possibility of its secession were again critical issues, he wrote:

> Quebec's existence helps us to express the difference between Canada and the United States. The U.S. is the melting pot; we are the mosaic. The U.S. is monocultural and officially unilingual. We are multicultural and officially bilingual. American Francophones are relegated to the bayous and backwaters of Louisiana, and pockets in New England. In Canada we have French immersion.[10]

Walkom's claims and the discourse that frames them were taken up by teachers at Maple Heights, though with considerably less confidence. For example, one teacher noted, "Compared with the U.S. we're gentle and inclusive, ever changing." Another teacher agreed with the importance of inclusion and stressed that "there is a need for commonality . . . commonality to bring the Black and Chinese together." However, this inclusion and transition also produced anxieties in the same teacher, who then claimed that "interest groups [are] whittling away at the mainstream culture." This trend was described as "dangerous" by the same teacher because "there is something wrong with mainstream culture as a collection of differences. The mainstream has to continue to exist. It can't be eroded completely. There is a problem of 'Canadian' defining itself. It is really hard to know these days what is right."

The difficulty of knowing what is right is made more complicated for this teacher, who enjoys being part of the multicultural city because of the diversity of neighbors and good ethnic restaurants. Here different cultures are a good thing if culture is consumable and nonthreatening. Ethnic restaurants do not appear to ask for much and offer pleasure. If nation could be unencumbered by ethnic presence, then there might be a state of social harmony. However, if there is to be a line drawn around what is imagined by nation because mainstream culture cannot be imagined as a collection of differences, then the ethnic presence must be seen as outside the nation. This is one of the paradoxes of the passion for identity in these times. It is also the consequence of a discourse of multiculturalism that is premised on an understanding of culture as a distinct set of attributes capable of distinguishing mainstream culture from minority cultures.

The 1970s in Canada, known as "the Trudeau years" because of Pierre Trudeau's premiership, have a strong hold on the popular imagination. Multiculturalism was at this time made official state policy, a development viewed by one teacher as being "good and bad." It was good because the popular image of "Canada the Good" was produced and promoted in this era. This is an identity of kindness, gentleness, and fairness both at home and abroad that this teacher willingly embraced. But he also saw this era as bad because, he claimed, its policies now mean that people "do not have to work anymore" and employment benefits "have taken away incentives." He spoke of being "bothered" because he believed these policies had "gone too far in undermining Canada." Now, he believed that he had to "change in order to teach to accommodate." The teacher explained, "I have to change to the twenty percent. We are not strong enough to say, 'This is Canada!'" He too summoned the United States, but in this instance as a good role model, an example of the kind of loyalty to the nation that Canada should be demanding of those who choose to live within its borders, rather than as a bad example. But Canada is also celebrated for being different from the United States, which is then construed as a bad role model: "We are known for our compassion and kindness as symbolized by the peacekeeping operations for which the country is known; for not beating our chests about how good the country is; for trying hard to be a caring society, especially towards the ethnic thing." However, it seems that there should be limits to Canada's caring toward "the ethnic thing": the same teacher cited a ruling by the Supreme Court of Canada that now allows Sikh Canadian members of the Canadian Mounted Police to wear their turbans as part of the uniform. This example was given to demonstrate how "the ethnic thing" is backfiring as "outsiders" are now "imposing their beliefs on us."

The anxieties expressed about the "bothering" present draw on the hierarchical and binary discourse of dominant and minority cultures. Here the dominant culture is perceived as under siege and threatened by minority cultures who compete for their places alongside the dominant. This sense of a struggle for the survival of the fittest is a different side of Bauman's "war on ambivalence." The dominant culture, often talked about in terms of the right to display Christmas trees and "English traditions," is conceived as particularly vulnerable and subject to being taken advantage of simply because the nation wants to be seen as caring and reluctant to "beat its chest." But here the ambivalence resurfaces: this teacher followed his pronouncements about outsiders imposing their beliefs on Canada with a pause and then said, "But maybe I'm wrong." This is an example of what Bhabha describes as a double narrative movement, a slide from one position to another.[11] Canada is applauded for being "good to its ethnics" and then "bad" for giving them too much, but then again, "Maybe I'm wrong." This final slide might have something to do with Canadian culture's elusiveness and the instability of its signifiers. The multicultural wars and their "war on ambivalence" allow the speaker to assert certainty one moment, only to find himself encountering doubt the next. Discourses clash and opposing feelings are juggled. This is a recurring practice in the making of identities, as we shall see in the chapters that follow.

The difficulties in pinning down culture are duplicated with respect to race, as illustrated in a conversation with a different teacher. This wa the teacher who made the case that "White students are now feeling excluded" by discourses of antiracism and multiculturalism. Having made that point he immediately went on to note that "Black is now 'in'." Black, he explained, is "fashionable" and therefore, "White students are also trying to become Black. There are White girls who are going out with Black guys but White guys don't like it." He did not say whether White boys were going out with Black girls and if so, whether Black boys or White girls approved or disapproved of that practice. However, his observation prompted him to recall a recent television talk show on the subject of kidney transplants which revealed that large numbers of Black people in the United States have kidneys donated by White people. This knowledge caused him to pause and quip that kidney transplants seemed to be making nonsense of the Black and White thing. It seemed that race was becoming increasingly difficult for him to pin down because of practices like dating, acting, dressing, and even changing kidneys across race. And yet, as we shall see more clearly in chapter 4, it is precisely these transgressions that make intelligible the boundaries of race.

Spoiled Identity

I have noted that talk of change, of what Maple Heights used to be and what it has become, is enmeshed in a multilayered discourse of nation, family, human rights, and fashions. The issue of violence is similarly entangled in this discourse. During my research at Maple Heights, school-based violence and violence among youth were popular subjects. This was a time when "zero tolerance" policies on violence in schools were talked about and calls for greater emphasis on law and order were made by politicians, even though statistics indicated that Toronto continued to be one of the safest cities in North America and that violent crimes had declined significantly.

Discourses of crime and violence circulated through Maple Heights. Many students with whom I talked spoke about "all the fights" in the school, frequently racialized as "between the different races," though few if any could provide any examples to support this claim. It seemed that Maple Heights was recovering from what Goffman calls a "spoilt identity" as a result of a shooting incident that occurred in the school in the late eighties.[12] The incident involved two people, one a twenty-nine-year-old mechanics student enrolled in the school's adult education program, the second a trespasser. A confrontation is alleged to have started between them outside the cafeteria, and then moved to the boys' bathroom, where the trespasser pulled a gun and wounded the student in the shoulder. The student was taken to the hospital and the trespasser to the police station. Though the local newspaper reported that "police do not think drugs were at the root of the dispute," and that "gangs and racism are also unlikely motives," the police were said to have noted, "There could be more than meets the eye."[13]

At the time of this incident, the school principal noted that this was "a rare demonstration of violence in a normally peaceful school." Despite the shooting's rarity, and the fact that there were no longer any students at Maple Heights who attended the school at the time of the incident, some insisted on referring to it as support for the claims about "all these fights" at Maple Heights. The obvious discrepancy between the reputation produced by the incident and what actually happens now in the everyday life of the school suggests the work of a "spoiled identity."

During the year I spent at Maple Heights there was a major conference organized for students at the school on the subject of violence. Here, the often racialized discourse of violence (as in references to students who have come from "war-torn countries" which "normalize violence" and to "big students in hooded jackets" who "can be intimidating") was contested by both teachers and students. Noted one teacher, "It is largely a myth but the ambiance leads you to recognize the potential for violence. It is the perception that gives credence to the problem." But one teacher noted that "the perceptions and the myths have to be balanced with the reality," and suggested that violence had become "normalized" by the media. This perception was given more credence in the academic year prior to the one I spent at Maple Heights when a second incident, allegedly involving two of the school's students, occurred in the shopping plaza not too far away. Then a former student from Maple Heights appeared before the City Television camera displaying a knife that, he claimed, was an example of what students had in their bags at Maple Heights. The individual was introduced not as a former student but as a current student of the school. Both administrators and students of Maple Heights were infuriated by the incident. A delegation of students appeared with public relations officers from the police force the same week in an attempt to correct the impression produced by the activities of the former student. However, the spoiled identity persisted. Students debated among themselves its effects and whether the impression was deserved or not. "It's all a myth," claimed one student who described the school as being safe "to the point of being wimpish." Nevertheless, a discourse of violence continues to mesh with discourses of race, youth, popular culture, immigrants, multiculturalism, antiracism, and standards in the construction of Maple Heights.

The discursive space of schooling, as the conflicting constructions of its past and present suggest, is rife with tensions. There is a desire among many teachers to know the many and varied cultures that students bring from other places. But alongside this desire to know is also a desire to be left alone so that one can continue in the imaginary old ways. The desire to know the different cultures and, conversely, the resentment toward having to know and adjust to them "in order to teach," as one teacher put it, are premised on an understanding of culture as a set of attributes that can be spatially and temporally defined and known. As this study will demonstrate, there is another meaning of culture that has to do with the ways that students work upon the imagined attributes and transgress the boundaries that attributes might otherwise sanction. Students produce new forms of culture, as well as race, and new cultural practices that facilitate their everyday social relations. The attributes of this other meaning of culture are elusive and changing. As we shall see in subsequent chapters, they can also be contradictory, as when the signifiers of race become fashion, including music and dress, or when White becomes Black,

Serbian becomes Spanish, and so on. My mapping of the discursive space of Maple Heights also suggests a relationship between teachers' nostalgia for the past and their present worries and anxieties about multiculturalism, anti-racism, and violence. In this relationship fantasies about history and the school are entangled with anxieties about the bodies that populate the institution. As we will note later, there is a gap between students and teachers in these kinds of conceptualization and the knowledge they produce.

3

Portraits of Identity

Maple Heights runs a program called "Positive Peer Culture" (PPC) that brings together groups of students to talk about social issues, personal interests, and concerns. Discussions are based on the principle of group counseling, which means sharing concerns and developing strategies for reflecting upon and dealing with the anxieties, problems, and dilemmas that are brought to the group. Students in the PPC are given a social studies credit toward their high school diploma. In the year I spent at the school, there were five such groups ranging in size from ten to fifteen students. One of the five was mixed but the other four were same-sex groups since, one of the teachers responsible for the program informed me, research suggests that students tend to communicate more readily and comfortably in same-sex situations. A teacher is assigned to work with a group, and students either enroll voluntarily, are recommended by a teacher, or are invited to join by a past or present member. Generally those recommended to the PPC are perceived as standing to benefit from the opportunities and structures for discussion afforded by the group.

47

I became involved in a number of PPC meetings on the invitation of some student members, and prior to participating secured the permission and agreement of all. I attended meetings of three groups, one mixed group and two same-sex. These meetings offered the opportunity to think about the conceptual underpinnings of "positive peer culture." Culture, in this context, refers to a set of values and principles that form a particular code of behavior. (Such a definition is reminiscent of the sociological definition discussed in chapter 1.) The code of behavior ideally protects students in their interactions with one another within and beyond the group. Members are expected to attend meetings regularly and maintain confidentiality, and are held responsible for what they have to say. Students are also required to respect cultural diversity and to challenge racism and sexism, for Positive Peer Culture is about social responsibility and developing sensitivity to the interests and differences of others. The wall charts in one of the discussion rooms offered guidelines for the culture the PPC promotes. One provided guidelines for what is termed "active listening," including being able to listen in ways that allow the listener to "reword the content" of what is heard and to "reflect the feelings" that are being expressed. (For example, students begin their interventions by stating, "What I'm hearing is . . . .") A second chart listed some of the impediments to good communication, which include tendencies to lecture, moralize, and resort to name-calling. A third chart summed up the philosophy of the culture that this organization promotes: people must care and show it; no one should hurt themselves or others; people can change; individuals must be accountable for their actions; behavior is bad, not people; problems provide an opportunity to learn.

Culture here is the set of principles that bind the adherents and those it hopes to win. It can be dispensed with or promoted, bought into or rejected. Either way, adherence to this culture has to be negotiated rather than imposed. One consequence of this ambivalent dynamic is that students are apparently free to talk about the issues that they might not be able to in other formal school settings. One teacher gave an example of the case of a student self-labeled "Greek," who shared her dilemmas about dating an older non-Greek, a topic which raised issues about relationships, age, ethnicity, and family expectations. In a second instance a male student concerned about the staring habits of another student invited this student to join his group to talk about this habit. The starer initially agreed but then changed her mind when she realized that she would be the only Black student in the group. However, this same student who did not want to be the odd one out racially complained about other students who make themselves "racially distinct" by wanting to sit together "as races."

These meetings also offered me the chance to meet and talk with students inside the group and beyond who seemed interested in my research project. In my initial meeting with the three respective groups, students were invited to introduce themselves. I offer my notes from these introductions as portraits of the students concerned. I use the concept of the portrait since these brief descriptions are only meant to capture a moment in a life, or a particular pose, and their likeness, as in any portrait, can be contested by the subjects they represent.

It is important to bear in mind that these introductions were made within a group. What was said was therefore shaped and influenced by the dynamics of the group. How students describe themselves may well be contingent upon how they think they are viewed by others, and how they might wish to be viewed and named. What is obvious, however, is that even as they name themselves, students are acutely aware of the limits to naming, as naming can never capture all that one wants it to. We need to be equally aware of the limits of these portraits and their attempts to capture in a single sitting something that is very complex and constantly shifting.

In the rest of this chapter I offer portraits of members of two PPC groups. In both cases there were some students who were absent from the group on this particular day. First I draw upon their introductions and then from more extensive one-on-one interviews with PPC members. In what follows I reconstruct the ways students introduced themselves within the two respective groups and present them as group portraits. This is followed by individual portraits that are drawn from more extensive one-on-one conversations that I had with PPC members.

Portraits of a Group of Male Students

Mario described himself as "Italian." He was born in Toronto and has never been to Italy but his parents are immigrants from southern Italy. As an Italian, Mario identified and mixed with "other Italians and Canadians" at Maple Heights and outside the school. Next to him sat Jack, a Black Canadian student, and I wondered if Mario's "Canadian" friends included Jack or others who look similar to him. "No," replied Mario, and explained that he was referring only to fourth and fifth generation Canadians. Mario saw himself as distinct from fourth and fifth generation Canadians because he himself is second generation Italian, but at the same time (and here we might recall the discourse of "Italians and immigrants" from the previous chapter) he was able to identify with these imagined earlier generations of Canadians, who he assumes do not include Blacks."

Jack sat wearing a pair of jeans twice his size, a huge jacket and a bright red bandana around his head, obvious signifiers of his passion for rap music and the hip-hop culture associated with it. With respect to how he wished to be identified, Jack was emphatic about being Canadian. His mother emigrated from Jamaica but, like Mario, he was born in Toronto. He described how his mother's emigration to

Canada was helped by a Chinese Jamaican woman who had earlier come to Canada. His mother was brought up by this woman back in Jamaica, which explains why she now "listens to reggae music while she is cooking Chinese food and is surrounded by Chinese things in the house." Consequently, how Jack, the well-known hip-hop student around the school, imagines "Canadian" and "Jamaican" and his place within these categories is not so easily reducible to simple notions of race or culture.

Rudolph emigrated to Canada from Jamaica at an early age and identified emphatically as "Jamaican." Since, in the next breath, Rudolph modified his identity position as "actually, Jamaican Canadian," the first claim might have been made in opposition to Jack's. He went on to talk about his passionate interest in being a deejay, which, he claimed, is a specifically Jamaican influence. He told us that he goes "back home" whenever he has the funds to do so, partly because going home allows him to keep track of what is happening in the Jamaican deejay world. This sense of home as "there" appears to be quite central to the friendships and relationships he forms "here." At Maple Heights, he told the group, he tends to both socialize and identify with other Jamaicans because they remind him of "the good old days back in Jamaica." "Here" seems to be made in relation to how "there" is imagined and remembered. However, while one might be useful for imaging the other, "here" and "there" also appear to collapse into each other as Rudolph seeks to play out what he might be like "back home" in the social relations that he enters into in this other home.

Suresh was the next to speak and he described himself, and those with whom he identifies, as "Brown." He emigrated from Trinidad ten years ago and immediately talked about what he described as "the problems with Trinidad." Other group members appeared surprised by the category *Brown* but disinterested in his account of the problem of drugs and crimes in which his family, he claimed, was implicated. I was curious about the lack of interest both in the category *Brown* and in "the problem." Outside the classroom one of the students explained that the lack of interest was because of Suresh's tendency to "talk big" and exaggerate. Claiming an identity in Suresh's case offers no guarantee of being taken seriously by those for whom the identity is articulated.

Delroy, the fifth to speak, was very clear about how he wanted to be recognized and named: "I see myself as just Black and proud of my background." He explained that he was proud of the achievements of Black people, but was unwilling to name or identify the people with whom he socializes. My curiosity was again aroused and in a later conversation Delroy expressed some ambivalence toward other students in the school who might lay claim to the same category as he does. "Tell you the truth, I keep my distance from them," he told me. Blackness, like Whiteness, is made up of a complex range of subject positions despite popular representations of it as "sameness." Delroy's claim to the identity category does not guarantee him intimacy with others who lay claim to the same category.

Hadji, the next person to introduce himself, was clearly very reserved and reluctant to speak at all. He did, however, eventually explain that he had emigrated with his parents and brother from Tunisia five years earlier. He shrugged his shoulders at the thought of laying claim to an identity category in the way that others had in their introductions. He did not lay claim to being African because the popular representations of Africa that circulate do not include the North. He also seemed reluctant to even name himself "Tunisian." Hadji turned out to be very much a loner as one of many relatively recent immigrants at Maple Heights. He did, however, have some curiosity about dominoes and frequently sat on the periphery of the domino table in the cafeteria quietly observing with interest and amusement.

Heinz seemed even more reluctant to take part in the

introductions. Like Hadji, he had emigrated five years earlier, but from Switzerland. He socialized only with his brother outside the classroom at Maple Heights. Though he had only been in Canada for five years, he appeared reluctant to embrace the category *immigrant*. Here we might recall the discourse that circulates at Maple Heights that marks the immigrant as visible. He did not fit that category. Heinz remained silent for the rest of the discussion.

Hon was the last member to speak and he described himself as "originally from Vietnam," but was careful not to name himself as "Vietnamese." He resisted the categories of race, ethnicity, or nationality that others in the group readily drew upon and insisted that working hard at school and playing badminton were his identity. He also elaborated on his interest in English literature. While in one sentence he insisted that he identified with other students in the school who were serious about work and play, "regardless of who they are," in the next sentence he spoke of keeping "mainly with Cambodian and Chinese students." He then quickly went on to talk about his love for the beat of rap music and hip-hop culture though he did not display any of the outward dress signs, as in the case of Jack above. Where, I wondered, might Hon stand in relation to a multiculturalist brand of "Vietnamese culture" or the Vietnamese student."

Portrait of a Group of Female Students

Franca was the first to speak in a group of six female students. Though she claimed to mix with "all kinds" in the school, was born in Toronto and had never been to Italy, she described herself as "proud to be Italian." It seemed in the company of her fellow non-Italian students, and specifically in her PPC group, Franca delighted in asserting an Italian identity (this was after all a discussion about identity). But this pride is also underpinned by ambivalence, for she then described her reception when speaking English in Italian shops: "They go, 'Look at her! She don't want to be Italian!'" Franca clearly took equal delight in asserting her command of English over her command of Italian and in "being Italian," and added that "the trouble with Italians is that they think they are 'it'" as if to affirm her mixed feelings toward the community (or at least the stereotypes by which she imagines it). Yet while she castigated Italians for thinking that they are "it," she also seemed to recognize that they think that she wants to be "it" when she refuses to speak Italian in their stores.

Marta immigrated to Canada from Serbia. Although she was a relatively new immigrant (five years resident in Canada), she did not see herself as Serbian. As she put it, "Well, you can't say you're Serbian these days." This was a time when the ethnic wars raging in the former Republic of Yugoslavia played themselves out as ethnic tensions in Toronto, including at Maple Heights. Next, to looks of disbelief from other students in the group, Marta announced that she saw herself as being "more Spanish." A Serbian immigrant laying claims to being Spanish? But this identity, "Spanish wanna-be" as one student later put it in the hallway, had nothing to do with national identity, with where she came from or the language she spoke. *Spanish* at Maple Heights is the category used to refer to Spanish-speaking students originally from Latin America and Marta closely identifies with this community. *Spanish* in this sense is a cultural category (in the next chapter we will see that it also becomes a racial category at Maple Heights) comparable to what in the United States is now called "Latino." For Marta and many of the other youth at Maple Heights it also refers to a particular mode of dress, a genre of music, and a specific style of dancing. We might recall here the teacher in the last chapter who observed that Black is now "in." For Serbian-born Marta, Spanish is the "in" category with which she chooses to identify.

Carol, a White student and the third to introduce herself, insisted that she is simply "Canadian." Her explanation for wanting to be recognized as Canadian and "nothing else" had to do with her discomfort with dual identity naming, as in "African Canadian." Pointing to the three other students present she announced that she did not see them as Black because that would mean that they were "loud and all the rest of it, and there is nothing bitchy about them." Curiously, no one in the group seemed perturbed by this obviously bad appeal to and reinscription of racist and gendered stereotypes. Carol was later described as "weird" and seemed a little alienated from the group.

Christine, our fourth student, seemed unusually shy and reluctant to speak. She did, however, explain that she was a very recent immigrant from Jamaica. While in one sentence she described herself as mixing with "all the different people" in the school, in the next she explained that most of her friends were Black, but added that this was not really about race, but more about the fact that they also came from Jamaica.

Eve emigrated from Ethiopia to Toronto six years ago. So outspoken a member of the group was she that when Marta explained the way she wanted to be seen, Eve interjected to ask how it was possible for people's identities to be tied up with how and where they danced. Introducing herself she declared, "I am Eve!"—which seemed a reaction to the overdetermining effects of identity categories. She continued, "I am not Black because black is like this!" She pulled at the pair of black slacks that she was wearing to suggest that black is a color and not a racial or political category. Eve then described her image: "People think I'm crazy and hot-tempered." She told of a Jamaican boy who had commented on her looks. To the amusement of the rest of the group she related how she had subsequently "sorted out" the situation. Eve identified very closely with her father, who "reads everything," but noted that even he found her a little tough at times.

Margaret, the last student in this unusually small group (several students had not attended the meeting), stressed that she was Black. She was born in Toronto of a Trinidadian father and a Jamaican mother. Having claimed the category *Black*, in the very next sentence she pointed out, "But there are many Black students in this school that I don't relate to at all." Like Delroy above, she is clearly attacking the practice of equating Blackness with sameness and thereby compromising the complexity of subject positions that might be taken up—even as she lays claim to this identity category. She made reference to what I read as pressure to conform and act in prescribed ways and then concluded, as if she were confronting a contingent of identity police, "Come on. Let me be what I want to be." Identity categories are thus claimed and resisted at the same time.

Portraits Discussed

Although these introductions are brief, they offer us a glimpse of the diverse backgrounds and the competing claims to identity of students at Maple Heights. Of the eight members of the first group, six are immigrants and the other two are children of immigrants. In the second group, four of the six are immigrants, a fifth is the daughter of parents from Jamaica and Trinidad, and the sixth traces her family to eastern Canada. These backgrounds remind us just how much of a diaspora space Maple Heights is, a space wherein individual subjectivities are forged not only through relationships with one another, but also through the multiple place associations that are invoked in their everyday encounters. Such associations are kept alive through first- and secondhand memories and through friendships. In these portraits immigrants from Ethiopia, Jamaica, Trinidad, Tunisia, Switzerland, and Serbia come together. These histories provide the grounds for diasporic identities, but always in relation to where one is now.

These diasporic identities are also changing under the conditions of globalization. For example, the deejay's friendships and career aspirations are intimately bound up with the trips that he makes "back home." On the other hand, the conditions of globalization and the changes in time-space that they suggest mean that "here" and "there" are often collapsed, so that, for example, Rudolph can "virtually travel" through television and the Internet. As these youths embrace and participate in the popular cultures that circulate globally, and as they make identifications with first- and second-hand memories of other places drawn from the family histories of migration, older assumptions about an immutable link between place, culture, and identity are undermined.

Popular youth cultures effectively defy the more rigid multicultural categories of race and ethnicity. For example, Hon can be Vietnamese and at the same time also belong to hip-hop culture, a move which both extends and transcends the meaning of *Vietnamese* while also challenging youth cultures as racial or ethnic property. Marta can be from Serbia and yet see herself as Spanish because *Spanish* is about music, clubs, and a mode of dress with which she identifies. In the process, identity categories like *Spanish* and *hip-hop* defer rather than displace *Serbian* and *Vietnamese*. The identity that is claimed always retains something of that other. Difference, in this sense, becomes what Derrida calls "differance," where difference meets deferral. In these situations where "chance meets necessity," both difference and identity become "strategic and adventurous," unlike official multiculturalism's rigid commodification of culture and lifestyles.[1]

The juxtaposition of introductions also reveals how relative and contingent is the process of making identity. Identity categories are frequently claimed in order to distinguish oneself from the perceived values and characteristics of others within the group. *Brown* emerges as a category to differentiate people with claims to a South Asian diaspora from those who might claim an African diaspora. This means that

the more totalizing category *Black*, which emerged as a political position in the sixties and seventies to encompass all
people of color in a shared political and social struggle, is
now fractured. However, as one student acknowledged, how
this new category *Brown* works can be confusing even for
those who lay claim to it. One Brown student told me that
Brown is the same as *Black* because both are the consequences and victims of racism and White supremacist attitudes. But he then invoked the discourse of resentment
noted in the last chapter, as he complained that the trouble
at the moment is that Blacks are now getting "all the attention," apparently at the expense of Browns. Desires here
seem split ambivalently between being the same and being
different.

Ambivalence might be so central to the process of making identities because of the inadequacies of identity categories in relation to lived experience, but part of the ambivalence also resides in the fact that identity may not always be
a matter of choice. Identities are here shaped by alienation,
racism, and a pervasive feeling of exclusion from the dominant culture. When categories are claimed, this might be
because they offer coherence and prevent discontinuities
from running rampant.[2] They remind us of the necessity of
identity. Despite this necessity, inside social groups difference is asserted in ways that challenge the disciplinary constraints of categorization. For example, the discourse of
"Blackness" may insist that there are prescribed ways of
being Black. And yet, as we see in these portraits, this practice also produces resistance on the part of those who lay
claim to the identity category, as with the student who
wanted to be Black but also wanted that category to allow
her to be what she wanted to be.

The work of postcolonial theorist Homi Bhabha is useful
for thinking about the anxieties of naming. He points out
that the "'Real Me' emerges initially as an assertion of the
authenticity of the person," but that the "'Real Me' as a state-

ment reverberates for the speaker as it becomes a question 'The Real Me?'" In this way the statement of identity becomes, in Bhabha's words, a question of identity.[3] The certainty that is invoked by "I am!" lingers momentarily and encounters doubt as it becomes "I am?" In other words, the very act of naming one's identity is also a moment of recognizing the limits to the name.

Larger Portraits

In the rest of this chapter, I discuss five narratives of identity drawn from more extended conversations with students from the mixed Positive Peer Culture group, Michele, Steve, Fred, Anna, and John. All the youth complicate definitions of culture as ethnic attributes, and take part instead in an urban culture characterized by hybridity, creolization, and flux. Canclini explains hybridization in terms of its key processes: the fragmenting and mixing of social collectives that used to organize cultural systems; the deterritorialization of cultural symbols and symbolic processes; and the expansion of impure cultural genres.[4] Not only is the elusive culture of these students shaped by such hybridity, what Hebdige named "cut 'n mix,"[5] but these youths are hybrid subjects in other ways. They occupy the space between childhood and adulthood. Many of the students with whom I spoke held part-time jobs, and were between the adult world of work and the adolescent world of high school. This cultural between space enables these youth to experiment and play in their identity work.

Michele: "More toward the Guyanese"

Although Michele was taking grade eleven courses at the time that we met, she had only been at Maple Heights for a year. Her grade nine and ten years were spent at a different school where, she hastened to note, "you could count the Black people and the minorities on one hand." Consequently she celebrates Maple Heights for its diversity and for "the whole mix thing that is going on." As she elaborated on "the mix thing," how to articulate what she saw and experienced became rather complicated. "I don't know how to explain it," she pointed out. "Students mix together, like in class and stuff, and that carries into the hallways but they don't necessarily hang out in groups. But there would be the odd one out." What Michele appears to have difficulty explaining here are the ways the boundaries of the cultures that exist at Maple Heights overlap and converge. What might be exoticized and marked out in theory as different cultures become inscriptions of hybridity in everyday social relations.

Michele described herself as "different from everybody else" because she "keeps to herself" and "follows her own style." In reality, however, Michele's presence in the school seemed anything but "keeping to herself." Her social relations tended to be with a group of largely male students whom she described as "the Spanish guys," who were "fun loving, easy going" and "not so serious." Because of certain discourses of ethnic identity, and specifically Black identity, she found it necessary to explain these relationships to me: "It's not because they are Spanish. I just find it easier to be with them." She continued, "When I first came here I started to hang around with the Spanish guys and I started to hear, 'Oh, Michele's a traitor,' or whatever. 'She doesn't hang with Black people,' or whatever." The discourse of identity categories can be used to discipline relationships and behavior, a situation complicated in this case by the competition, elaborated in chapter 4, between two marginal groups.

Michele's mother and father emigrated respectively from Jamaica and Guyana. She claimed to be "more toward the Guyanese" while her brother is "more toward the Jamaican." Asked to elaborate on this distinction she explained that her brother was considered a "roots" person, one who is more interested in reggae and dance hall music, while she claims to be "more into the hip-hop thing." She also listened to Bhangra music, a fusion of Bengali, rap, and reggae. Ethnic distinctions here collapse into popular culture choices, but even these distinctions are difficult to sustain. When her brother spent time with Michele and she played her tapes, "He goes, 'Turn it up! Turn it up!'" Meanwhile, in their household the parents' musical collection included "the really old reggae stuff, calypso, people like Nat King Cole and church music."

These images of multiple converging and intertwining sites of identity were duplicated outside the home. On the bus to school Michele connected up with three friends she described as Black, and a pregnant White student who seemed to value her support. Friends in her first class of the day included one she described as "Guyanese East Indian." Michele was unable to offer any details beyond these racial-ized categories, which might speak to the influence that race commands in her everyday social relations. On the other hand she might have thought these were the kinds of responses the ethnographer expected.

Michele's second class of the day was drama, which she liked because "you get to express yourself. You don't have to be 'you' for a whole period. You can just be a whole differ-ent person." Drama gave her the legitimate opportunity to suspend the everyday expected ways of behaving and to experiment with a range of imagined identities. Michele felt quite close with one student in the group: "Like, she is the White version of hip-hop. Me and her get along because we have so much in common." When drama was over, Michele could be seen bantering with her Spanish friends in the hall-way, but then she spent some time in the library with a friend described as Polish and with a newly arrived student from Jamaica whom she described as "a very independent sort of person." Her social relations appeared to be stretched across the racial and ethnic spectrum at Maple Heights.

I wondered how Michele saw herself benefitting from Positive Peer Culture. She rattled off instances of the kinds of issues they had discussed: someone who had talked about coming close to suicide, which she thought was an attempt to be noticed; a family abused by the father; and one whose family does not love her. Michele felt that PPC had taught her to listen to people more openly, to try to find out how they were feeling, and to work from there. Most importantly, she felt she was learning to control her anger.

Steve: "They Call Me 'Wigger'"

Steve, an eighteen-year-old youth at Maple Heights, was also a member of the mixed-gender PPC group to which Michele belonged. He described himself as in grade twelve doing grade nine courses, because he had not performed particularly well in his previous years. He also described himself as not having any real interest in school, although he felt his attitude was getting better. "It's not the school itself," he noted. "Let's say it's some of the teachers and different things about teachers here." But in the next sentence Steve acknowledged his propensity for getting himself in trouble and related an incident that had occurred that morning. When his friend asked for a cigarette he took one from his packet, whereupon he was reprimanded by the teacher who "started yelling. Like, I'm not supposed to have cigarettes." He challenged the teacher on this rule: "I go, 'Where is this rule coming from?' And she made me read my code of behavior book. It said no smoking in or on school property, right? And I said, 'I'm not smoking.' She sent me to the office because of my attitude." Apparently Steve took delight in this challenge to school authority. I wondered how it related to the culture of PPC. Steve shrugged his shoulders, clearly recognizing the contradictions between the pleasure he got from this moment of defiance and what the Positive Peer Culture required of him.

Steve was very quiet in his PPC group. He told me that he had not brought "too many things" to the group because "nothing really that much happens in my life." The one incident he had brought to the group concerned an arrest for assault, but since the whole thing had been sorted out he claimed he was not even sure why he brought this up. During lunch breaks he could be seen smoking a cigarette in an area of the parking lot where a group self-identified as Guyanese often congregate. When not in this area, he told me, he spends his time at the local community center playing basketball. He chose to play there rather than in the school partly because he did not feel particularly close to those who play ball in the school and partly because the hoops at the center were low enough for him to be able to dunk the ball.

Steve did not lay any claim to ethnic identity. He was born in Windsor, Ontario, and while he noted some French background in his roots he seemed totally disinterested in exploring this background. Since the age of seven he had lived in an area of Toronto, not too far from Maple Heights, known to be very diverse ethnically. He claimed that if he were to be identified with any group at school it would be the Guyanese group. He grew up listening to both reggae and rap music. His mother listened to reggae although, he noted, she was unable to understand all of the language in the way he could. He rattled off the list of rap artists he currently listened to and described the hip-hop dress mixed with "roots" that he tended to wear. Then, in a moment of ambivalence toward these specific signifiers, he told me that he was changing his style: "They [the people with whom he identified] dress like hip-hop, but with jeans and stuff. I use to, [but] I'm getting sick of it. I understand the ripped jeans are a style. I wear those baggy black jeans but I don't wear the colorful pants so much." The ambivalence seemed to come from the "policing" effects of many of the identity categories that abound at Maple Heights, and the desire to be both the same and different. He continued, "I'm changing my style because too many people are doing that now." Doing what? I wondered. "Like calling people 'wigger'," Steve continued with an uncomfortable and resigned laugh. "You know. That means 'white nigger'." He hastened to explain that what he identified with was what he had grown up with and noted with a giggle, "They call me Snow. You know, the singer, right?" (Snow is a renowned White Canadian rap artist.) Talking about social groups in the school, he continued, "People stay with their own because they know people from where they live or from the schools they were at before. It's not really about Blacks with Blacks. They're just friends."

Steve's social networks transgressed the boundaries of race and ethnicity one moment and reinforced them the next. He forms social relationships around what is named "Black popular culture," but he is then labeled "wigger" and so becomes "fed up" and begins to change his style and the social relations that accompany it. The nature of these shifting networks is akin to Chambers' notion of networks that emphasizes continual involvement in the active processes of networking in such a way that the network is like any other net, "full of holes, of openings, of possibilities."[6] The openings and possibilities of these postmodern networks have less and less to do with where Steve is from and more to do with where he finds himself now. In other words, the social relations that help form the identities of Steve and other youth like him have more to do with "routes," the various trajectories, interactions, and networks through which these youth are connected, than with "roots," or countries of origin, birthplaces, and ethnicity.[7] Again we see that the culture that they are in the process of making through these interconnections transcends the ethnic absolutism often invoked by antiracist and multiculturalist discourses.[8] But these processes are not without tension, as the name calling suggests.

Fred: "Black but Canadian. Period!"

Fred's narrative drew on a remarkably similar discourse of how the different cultures mingle and then diverge at Maple Heights. The thing that Fred particularly liked about Maple Heights was that "the cultures that come to this school can be separate among their own people and not have to fuss with anybody." He thought individuals who identified and kept within ethnic groups were "alright" because "I'm sure that nobody has anything against any other race. There's one or two that's like the bad apple in each group. But I'm sure it's like not a problem for anybody because everybody is with their own group." He went on to affirm, as did the other students above, that students cross the boundaries of these groups at specific moments, only to return to them at others.

Fred is very tall and was wearing a large, loose fitting jacket, a combination he thought invoked a certain stereotype of the threatening Black male. He was concerned about this and about other ways Black students were treated differently from White students, as in the example of the Black student skipping classes who is noticed in a way that "some Italian, White, or Jewish person is not." But then he also claimed that Black students chose stupid places to hang around when they were skipping class. "If you were to walk out to the parking lot you'd see how much people skip there." I asked if the students in the parking lot included Black students. Fred replied "No. You can't play dominoes outside!" Here he mocks the image of the domino-playing Black student but also those students who choose to play dominoes in the cafeteria instead of attending their classes. Conversely he might be mocking the practice of not skipping skillfully. He was also very critical of the overt and covert ways that racism works at Maple Heights and of the subtle codes of new racism. But he refused to view Black subjects as innocent and singled out The African Queens, whom we will meet in chapter 5, for criticism:"They say we should stick together as Black people and have friendships. I never take them seriously because they talk one thing and do another."

Speaking about all the different identities that might be claimed at Maple Heights, Fred expressed frustration with the discourse of new racism that constructs Canadian as White and in the process positions him outside. On this he was most passionate:

> I say I'm Canadian. They go, "No you're not. You're Jamaican. You have Jamaican parents. Right?" . . . Like, so what if I have Jamaican parents? That does-n't make me Jamaican. I'm Canadian. Period. So it sort of upsets me when people say I'm Jamaican and not Canadian, because I don't feel Jamaican and I'm not Jamaican. I'm Canadian with Jamaican descent or background.

Fred vacillates between inscribing and fighting stereotypes. "Black identity would have to do with music," he claims, but then refuses to limit himself to the racialized music categories that dominate at Maple Heights, saying, "I'm just a music guy. Everything. Jazz and all." He is a dedicated member of the Pentecostal Church, where his religious commitments and his musical tastes come together.

Anna: "Just Canadian"

A fourth member of this PPC group, seventeen-year-old Anna, was born in Newfoundland and moved to Toronto at the age of ten. She identified herself as "just Canadian." In the same way that we see students in the portraits above negotiating a sense of self in relation to another "home," Anna's identity was also considerably shaped by her ongoing connections with relatives in Newfoundland. Unlike her cousin there, who was surprised by Anna's yearbook because although she had seen Chinese and Black people, "she has never seen anyone else," Anna celebrated the multicultural mix of Maple Heights. But like so many students there, while she likes to be a part of this mix, she also blamed it for what she described as "all the fights among the different races." However, when asked for details of "all these fights," Anna too struggled. At first she thought the fights were between "the Italian guys and the Pakistani guys," but then she changed her mind and thought they might be between Italians and Blacks. Then, it became evident that she was not exactly clear what people made up the Pakistani group. We stayed on the subject of fights, and Anna recalled an incident involving her brother who, she claimed, "had been involved in so many fights" before he graduated the previous year. Details of these fights were vague, but what became clear was that what started off as being "fights between all the races" were now fights between her brother and his contemporaries, and since those involved were neither Black nor Pakistani, fighting was no longer a racialized phenomenon. Whiteness, as Dyer reminds us, becomes that space for anything and nothing.[9] Fights are imagined as "between the races" or "between different cultures" when those involved are identified as Spanish, Black, or Vietnamese. But they become "just fights" when the parties involved are described as White.

Anna liked to participate in her PPC group although she explained that she had brought very few items to the group herself. She valued the opportunity to listen and talk with people who often brought in difficult issues, hinting at people's tendency to discuss relationships with the opposite sex. She had a special closeness with a student named John (whom we will meet below) who "never put anybody down" and was a "really nice guy." The special relationship forged with John extended beyond the PPC group as the two often talked to each other in the evenings by phone.

On the question of identity, Anna observed that she is a White Canadian, "just like Fred is a Black Canadian, or

African Canadian or whatever." She went on to explain, "Black and White are the main people and there are the Pakistani people and Chinese people in the middle of everybody. It's like they're now the minority." This observation drew upon the majority/minority discourse noted among teachers in the previous chapter, in which some receive more attention than others. The category *Brown* for Anna appears to encompass a wider range of groups than it does for the student who introduced the concept above, including students who come from Somalia and Ethiopia. She explained that this categorization had to do with the size of the group and what she perceived as their relative isolation: "Yes. I'd put them with the Brown people because there are not many of them. Like, the Black people don't hang with them and the White people don't hang around with them. So they're kind of like, to each other. But I don't know." Like the teacher in the last chapter, Anna expressed her doubt about what she knew.

John: "Hard and Soft Racism"

John was born in Toronto but at the age of six was sent to live with his grandmother in Jamaica. When he was fifteen his grandmother died and he returned to live with his mother in Toronto. He believed that going to live with his grandmother in Jamaica instilled in him a different set of values and said of a friend brought up in Toronto, "The way he talks to his mother I could never have dreamt of speaking to my grandmother. And his ancestors come from Jamaica." But while his memories of living with his grandmother in Jamaica are clearly sweet, he also questions the wisdom of his mother sending him there to live in the first place. He now sees his mother "more as a relative, and a very close relative, but not in the real mother sense." His ambivalent reflections remind us of the process of splitting and splicing that is central to the making of culture and identities, in this case between Jamaica and Toronto, within a diaspora space.

John is very explicit about identifying strongly "with the Black roots" which "in a word is being proud." At the time of our conversation the first multiracial elections were taking place in South Africa and he described "see[ing] all the differences coming out of South Africa" as an indication of the larger framework within which his pride is constituted and the seemingly geographically distant influences that act upon it. Despite his "Black pride" John expressed little interest in laying claim to a notion of some fixed Black culture, distant or otherwise. For example, while John described himself as Black (he is what many students describe as "light-skin Black") he hastened to add that he was "also a mixture of Indian and White." I enquired whether John was interested in exploring these aspects of his roots. "No," he stressed, "because even in the mixture there is a mix!"

The metaphor of "mix" appeared to structure the social relations that John formed around the school. He combined his dress in ways that defy the popular cultural categories of *roots, hip-hop, Black,* and *White.* During the lunch periods he could be seen playing cards with a group of students whom he referred to as "the United Nations" but noted, "They are students with the same kind of values." He elaborated, "There are people who come from the same place as me but are totally different from me." He also gave what became a very familiar response to my question to students about what they liked about the school: "The mixture that is here." He cited the Jamaican national motto, "Out of many, one people," in support of his claims. About the ways areas of the cafeteria and the corridors appear to be racially designated spaces he said, "There are areas that are White. There are areas that are Black. [But] there are so many people that I can feel comfortable with. There is no way that I am going to say, 'Shall I go here or not? Am I going to fit in or not?' . . . Color is not a wall."

Despite John's friendships and community, which could not be readily reduced to either race or ethnicity, he was very aware of the rigid ways that his body is read and the racist practices that stem from this reading. He described the subtle or "soft" ways by which racism is practiced, including a special tone of address, differential treatment that might not be so easily identified as discriminatory, and readings of his body as culturally different. For instance, John described a teacher who would "get more excited when I ask a question. 'Why ask that? Why wasn't I paying attention?' Students of the same color as she was would just get the answer and carry on."

I asked John for an example of what he calls "strong racism." "When you actually have evidence. Like her actually making reference to my color," he replied. *Soft racism* thus parallels new racism, which appeals to cultural metaphors and may never mention race, while *hard racism* is akin to the scientific racism which makes crude appeals to biological differences. But John's examples also show us how the former retains elements of the latter since new racism continues to read the body.

Portraits and Identity

These portraits of a few of the students at Maple Heights suggest some of the complexity of the work of identity for youth. While all of the Black students spoke of experiences of racial discrimination, they also all refused to confine identity concerns to the discourse of victims. This reminds us that identity cannot be addressed simply in terms of oppression and victimization. Other youths in these portraits who see themselves, or who might be seen by others, as "ethnics" lay claim to ethnicity in contradictory and ambivalent ways: born Serbian but identifying Spanish; proud to be Italian but also proud to defy Italians by speaking English; South Asian and Brown; and both different from and the same as Black. Then there are those who see themselves as neither racial nor ethnic subjects but nevertheless make relationships to the racial and ethnic signifiers that are available. These attributes are not those of the official discourses of multiculturalism and ethnic distinctiveness, but rather the popular cultures of youth that are constantly changing.

The complexity of identity work demonstrated in these portraits also confirms the difficulty noted in the first chapter of separating the dynamics of identity from those of culture and race. Many of the signs and symbols of the popular cultures of these youth, like dress codes and musical tastes, are racialized. This means that the signifiers of race can also change with the changing signs of culture and identity, and what it means to be a certain race is different from one context to another. Consequently, since culture is racialized but not fixed in bodies, racial identities are also more open. However, as noted, discourses may both facilitate and constrain identity, and there is a tension between the opportunities for playing with the racial signifiers and the need for stable group identities. The tensions may invoke strategies for policing identity and determining who can belong and who is alienated. The creation of a new exclusionary category, *wigger*, might be one such example.

These portraits also show us some of the tensions arising from the intersection of two complementary and competing understandings of identity outlined in chapter 1, essentialist beliefs in fixity, and the constructivist conception of identity as process. The instances that I have cited, following Bhabha, to show how identity may be announced as a statement of "I am," only to become the question "I am?" demonstrate how the notion of identification helps us to better understand the process of making identity. Identification refers to the complex dynamic that brings identity into being as individuals name themselves, but at the same time naming calls that very identity into question and makes it a problematic.[10] Identity categories and labels are often unable to satisfy the desire to be recognized as complex subjects. Identity is therefore always partial, capable of telling us something but unable to tell us all.

Despite the difficulty of separating the dynamics of culture, race, and identity, I have tried to make culture the central question of this chapter. In the following chapter I pay more explicit attention to the dynamics of race. While the content of the conversations drawn upon in the next chapter might be somewhat different from the present chapter, the structure of discourses of culture and race are similar. As we shall see, the tension produced as youth simultaneously invoke the similitude or sameness of cultural identity and the difference within that identity is also also echoed in students' talk of race.

4

Talk of Race and Identity

At the end of an OAC law class that had centered on the relationship of law to culture and identity, two male students (one of whom had remained silent throughout the discussion) approached me, clearly intent on continuing the discussion that had just taken place. Both students, now aged eighteen, had returned to Maple Heights to complete their high school education after having dropped out of school for a year. "This place is so different now," pointed out the student who had remained silent during the class discussion. "Not like it used to be. So different," he repeated. "How is it different?" I asked. "Look. Look around you," he replied in a lowered voice. I pointed out that since I was new to Maple Heights I had no picture of the past with which to compare what I saw. At this point in the conversation we were walking along a hallway crowded with students changing classes. I asked him again to tell me how the school had changed. Nodding in the direction of a small group of Sikh students who were distinguished by the turbans they were wearing, he exclaimed,

> Well, look! Now you have all these cultures. All these different groups. Especially the Spanish students. All

these groups keeping together. It used to be different. There used to be Italian students. Italians and Blacks. Right? And the Blacks used to be OK. The Italians used to hang out in the parking lot because the Italians got the cars, right? Man, there used to be at least a hundred of us out there. Now you'll be lucky if you find ten. Now you got all these groups and people keeping to their cultures. Especially the Spanish. And look there. [A White student wearing a bandana around his head was drinking at the nearby fountain.] That's what I can't stand. People trying to be like other people's cultures.

While a White student wearing a bandana became a cultural anomaly, this student then reflected upon a previous experience that challenged these notions of ethnic and cultural distinctiveness:

But then again, look at Bena. This is the guy that used to come to this school. Bena is White. Like I mean *White* White. But you know he grew up with them and so he is like *real Black*. He talk like them exactly and he dress real Black. I mean he is *real* Black. Yeah. But me and him [his friend], we're Italian, man! Nothing but!

A week after this conversation, in which the bandana became the signifier of "other people's culture" and where "*white* White" became "*real* Black," I was in conversation with a grade ten student named Nita. She and I had chatted on more than one occasion in the hallways and in the drama studio. Nita had already identified herself as being from the Dominican Republic, and so we talked about the events that were unfolding in neighboring Haiti at the time. This desire to know more about what was happening "at home" was striking for demonstrating how developments there helped her to make sense of her new identifications and social relations in Toronto. As this particular conversation progressed, talk of race in Haiti gave way to talk of race and culture in Toronto. Nita had emigrated from the Dominican Republic one year earlier. Her curly hair and brown complexion are generally characterized as "Black." For Nita, however, this category *Black* was incompatible with *Spanish*, which is the identity she embraces. "Some of these students, they make me mad!" Nita told me. She explained:

> They don't know anything about Dominica. They say to me, "You Jamaican?" I tell them, "No, I'm not Jamaican. I'm not Black. Can't you tell? Can't you hear my accent? I'm Spanish, not Black!"

Nita's contested position within Maple Heights—who she feels she is, versus how her body is read—lies somewhere between her history and the dominant discourses of race, culture and ethnicity that prevail at Maple Heights. In the Dominican Republic there are more categories of race than in Toronto. Since the meanings of race are not universal, the signifiers of race that fourteen year old Nita brings with her have to be renegotiated in relation to the new meaning of race and culture she encounters at Maple Heights.

I relate these two moments of students' talk of race and identity because they suggest something about the contradictory, transgressive, and ambivalent ways students live their lives in relation to the circulating discourses of race, ethnicity, and culture. Momentarily, the student who sees himself as "Italian and nothing but" is able to read culture onto the bodies that populate the hallways of Maple Heights. Groups of students become "all these different cultures." When bodies are read in this way, the theoretical distinction between race and culture falls down. In the next moment, however, the case of Bena confirms the Italian's view that race is about cultural affiliations and therefore reminds him of the dangers of reading bodies too rigidly around the school. One moment he identifies with the discourse that sees the student wearing a bandana as an anomaly; the next he recalls the lived experiences of another student which makes that discourse problematic.

The background for the two moments cited and for the conversation that I draw upon in the rest of this chapter is a social landscape that is littered with a range of stereotypes and metaphors for race, culture, and identity. This landscape is a hazy one because those who populate it are also continually contesting and displacing its stereotypes and metaphors. This haziness can be a source of anxiety, as for those teachers who romanticize how things used to be. But as is the case with the first student above, the appeals to fixity begin to dissipate when they are brought to bear on how things are. It is against this landscape of dissipating race and elusive culture that identifications are precariously carved out, and positionalities claimed.

The rest of this chapter is a detour through this landscape. My use of "landscape" follows Appadurai's, in which "scape" captures the fluidity of the categories and the shifting perspectives through which they are perceived.[1] A number of questions structure the discussion: How are color categories of race such as *Black*, *Brown*, and *White*, or geographic and historic ones like *African*, *South Asian*, *Oriental*, and *European* imagined, articulated, and contested at Maple Heights? How do discourses of race as fixed converge with the everyday practices of making race? What does it mean to think about race as relational and contingent?

Different Cultures/New Racism

When the student above points to a group of Sikh students at Maple Heights as evidence of "all the different cultures," he equates culture with ethnicity. "Normal Canadians" (meaning White) see themselves as different from those who are saturated by culture (meaning ethnic). (We will encounter the concept of "normal Canadians" in more detail later in this chapter.) One consequence of this popular discourse is that specific groups, in this case Sikh students, are perceived as saturated by culture and symptomatic of "the problem of all these cultures." As indicated in chapter 2, this impression produces the perception of the "multicultural wars" and beliefs about "them" imposing "their" culture on "us." Culture, in this sense, is seen as pathological and infectious, though the cultures of others can also be objects of desire for those who see themselves as "normal" or "without culture." There is something ironic about this reading of culture, particularly in a context where multiculturalist discourses prevail. While many individuals perceive different cultures as a problem, they also tend to say that the good thing about Maple Heights is that it has "all these cultures" of which the school can be proud and should celebrate. This situation becomes doubly ironic because those who talk about the need to celebrate difference, as in cultures and races, frequently see themselves as the "normal Canadians" who either "lack culture" or keep it private. In other words, their culture is normalized. This contrasts with those who are perceived as publicizing their culture by wearing it on their bodies and, in the process, segregating their cultural and racial selves.

The two students in the first episode above, unlike those they read around the school as embodying "all the different cultures," find themselves in the enviable position of being able to be "Italian and nothing but" and then, under other circumstances, capable of converging with the dominant category *White* to become *normal Canadian*. Recall here how the population of Maple Heights was constituted by one of its teachers as changing in the 1980s from "eighty percent Italian" to "eighty percent immigrant." The visible (as in "visible minorities") Sikhs in turbans, Blacks in large parkas, and Spanish with bandanas around their heads, on the other hand appear to resist assimilation. Furthermore, the visible immigrants are also stigmatized by the populist discourses (noted in chapter 2 and frequently reproduced by students in conversation with me) that lump immigrants together with questions of law and order, jobs, welfare, social disintegration, and so on. Consequently, these students live the burden of representing stereotyped and stigmatized cultures while having to fight against them at the same time.

"Paki" is a derogatory shortcut name for people from Pakistan. However, at Maple Heights "Paki" is also used to lump together anyone with claims to South Asian origins. This means that even Sikhs and others who come not from Pakistan but from other countries such as India and Sri Lanka are labeled "Pakis." Such students are frequently constituted as far removed culturally from everyone else at Maple Heights, and become Bauman's "strangers among us."[2] The "unredeemable sin" of such strangers, according to Bauman, is that they upset and challenge the reliability of the conventional landmarks and the social ordering simply because they are physically close and yet appear spiritually remote. Their presence is consequently seen as incompatible with the fundamental order of the social world.[3] Although Bauman's concept need not be limited to those insultingly labeled "Paki," this specific section of the Maple Heights community appeared to be doubly marked as strangers since they tended to keep to themselves. Talking about what he identified as "the Pakistani Group," a student who identified himself as "normal Canadian" observed:

> They don't cause any trouble. They just do things among themselves. There are people that I know, but they're not my friends, who I hear talk about the guys with turbans. They call it "punch bag" and all that. But my friends don't make fun of them. Not that much. I guess sometimes, though. But not that much.

Here Sikh students with turbans are mistakenly named "Pakistani" and made the object of ridicule. This student struggles within multiculturalist discourses: different cultures are ridiculed rather than celebrated, but the frequency of the making fun shifts from "sometimes" to "not that much."

New racism draws upon these codes of culture and difference. These students "don't cause any trouble" and yet the way these students are singled out as "sticking together" is seen as "the trouble." In a different conversation the familiar claim was made that "it is not that I have anything against immigrants, but they should at least be able to speak English." In the next sentence the same student identified "Pakistanis" as responsible for her mother's four years of unemployment. This she claims to know because these "facts" are also "common sense." Constituting "common sense" in this manner is, again, a symptom of new racism. Such prejudicial perceptions are presented under the guise of reported speech: other people do and say these things. New racism also suggests a model of *racial descent*, an evolutionary scale in which the Other, resisting assimilation and upsetting notions of social cohesion, appears to walk backwards into deviancy. I will return to this concept of racial deviance later in the chapter. Important to note for now, however, is that this particular model of new racism assumes that if one balances insults about the Other by also speaking positively of the group (that they "keep together," have a "good culture," and "don't cause any trouble"), then one is not racist. Instead, one is reasonable and describing things as they are.

We might note that groups within Maple Heights occupy different places on this evolutionary scale of racial descent, but that some positions are more fixed than others. Black students, for example, have a more fluid location on the scale than those constituted as "Paki." This observation does not suggest that one group is racialized more than the other, or that one is the greater victim of racism than the other.

However, recalling that "Black is 'in'" (chapter 2) and that anyone can become Black in Black popular culture (chapter 3), the identity of "Paki" appears more rigid. This rigidity, however, is not universal to all students who are immigrants or children of immigrants from various countries of South Asia, including Pakistan. It does not extend to the Pakistani and other students at Maple Heights with closely cropped hair and pierced ears who walk around the school listening to Bhangra music. Bhangra and its fusion of Bengali music with roots and hip offers opportunities for identity crossing and mutations. Identification with Bhangra can become another variant of "cool" and of what is "in," while the multiculturalist variety of culture as religious difference, foods, and traditions is a less acceptable site of difference.

"Normal Canadians"

Two grade eleven students who identified themselves as "normal Canadians" had difficulty explaining what their culture was all about, though they were able to point out that they "ate normal food like steak." Both declared their interests in rock music but were keen to distance themselves from the "regular" and more readily recognizable rock group at Maple Heights, whom they identified as wearing tight jeans, having long hair, and often smoking outside the school during lunch breaks. In our conversation both were anxious to insist that they had "no problem with other cultures, especially the Blacks." Marcus, one of these two students, then added that the problem now was that "they" were now being racist towards "us." Among the incidents cited in support of this claim, two were memorable. One involved, as Marcus put it, "this big Black girl" who obstructed his entrance to the classroom and insisted on hurling insults at him. In the other a female student attacked him with her water pistol. Had these students looked like him, things might have been different, but the fact that they were females and Black meant that the incidents became gendered and racialized. The actions of the student with her water pistol and the one blocking the doorway became incidents that made whole sections of a community racially deviant. However, in separate conversations, both friends were insistent that Black people, or at least those "that one can talk to," are alright.

In the complex and contradictory discourses that structure these conversations, students' decisions about what is appropriate and, in contrast, deviant behavior, shape their attitudes toward race. If, it seems, one can be spoken to and engaged in conversation then one is racially normalized. On the other hand behavior of "the other race" that is met with disapproval (blocking entrances or harassing with a water pistol) is made racially deviant. In this process of differentiation, culture can be disarticulated from race one moment and, when cultural practices are perceived as displeasing, racialized the next. The students who have "nothing against other cultures" become irritated by students who they perceive segregate themselves by wearing the Malcolm X symbol. Blacks are now "racist," and in the following statement, ignorant: "I know it's their culture but then I don't know how much they know about it." Students who display what is then imagined as their culture cannot be engaged in quite the same way as those who keep their culture private or, whose culture is "normal" (as in "normal Canadian"). "Normal culture," according to this discourse, is in fact indiscernible (except when its food is compared with "ethnic food") because, as Richard Dyer notes, whiteness can be a space for anything and nothing.[4] Even as these claims are made, however, certainty meets doubt and ambivalence. Marcus, for example, identifies other cultures, notably Black students, as the ones who are always starting the fights and who "have the big attitude," but he ends his assertions about these Others with "maybe." He added that the same attitude goes for the Spanish students and then again added, "maybe," rather like the teacher in chapter 2 who contended multiculturalism is bad for Canada and then reflected that "maybe" he was wrong about his assertion.

A number of contradictory sentiments appear to be at work in the perceptions, claims, and counterclaims to which I draw attention above, but two stand out. One is the desire to distinguish race and culture so that one can engage in shared cultural interests that transcend race and ethnicity. This appeared difficult at Maple Heights as culture and cultural practices were frequently racialized. There is also a desire to assert identities as unencumbered sets of cultural attributes, but this is also difficult because the social relations and identities that are formed around culture (and popular culture) are always shifting. These are the tensions through which race is lived.

Racialized Subjects

In the rest of this chapter, I consider further how these dynamics are lived in the stories of five students. Margaret and Trevor are Black and were both born of Caribbean parents in Toronto. They do not know each other. José is Spanish, which in effect means that his first language is Spanish. He is originally from El Salvador. Gio identified himself as Italian and was born in Toronto to parents who are immigrants from the south of Italy. Gio should have appeared in one of the portraits in the last chapter but was absent for the Positive Peer Culture class of that day. (Gio was, in fact, frequently absent.) Jane, the fifth student, is White, but unlike the two students above who self-identified "normal Canadian," Jane is more conscious about a politicized White identity. She was in fact a self-identified and unapologetic supporter of the White supremacist movement and had until relatively shortly before my interview been a member of the Heritage Front, a right wing organization known for its racist views. For all of these students I provide a very brief sketch of their family backgrounds and of their diasporic roots and connections. This is because the memories and fantasies of other places and of dispersed family histories affect perceptions of race in very specific ways.

The tensions of race and identity suggested in these conversations are partly the effects of fixing race in discourse while it is lived as fluid and shifting. This is paralleled by the tension between the discourses of culture as inheritable attributes and group property and the more elusive ways by which youth are continually making and remaking culture and their identities. The focus in this chapter differs slightly from the portraits offered in the last chapter because here I pay specific attention to the discourses of race that inform and shape these conversations.

Trevor

Trevor was an eighteen-year-old student who was born in Toronto to Jamaican parents. He had only recently come to join Maple Heights in order to complete his final high school courses so that he could go on to university. Prior to coming to Maple Heights he attended a Catholic high school. Luigi, Trevor's close friend, also came to Maple Heights from the same Catholic School. They have known each other since grade five. When I first met them studying in the library during lunch, they told me they were both set on going to university.

The most important person in his life, Trevor told me, is his mother. "If it wasn't for my mother," he began and then paused. "Well she has taken care of me. I had three brothers. They lived in Jamaica and she worked hard to bring them all up here one at a time. I see all the struggle she has gone though and one day I hope that I can give back to her what she has given to me. She is very important." His mother, he claimed, is "more Jamaican" than many Jamaicans. His mother speaks "Jamaican" at home and although he can understand it he tends not to speak to her in the same language. He added, "My brothers, we can talk to each other in Jamaican sometimes but mostly in English. They can speak the language better than I can. They can go both ways."

"How do they feel about you not speaking the language as well?" I asked. Trevor replied promptly and defensively, "Oh, I do as well. Like there is no real problem. If I say something in Jamaican they look at me like, 'Oh! Like there is some culture in you!'"

The culture that is in Trevor, however, is socially ambiguous. The symbols and materials that provide the cultural identity he imagines as Jamaican—language, musical tastes, clubs—are not simply a constraining network of traditions, beliefs, and practices through which he is disciplined and produced. Instead, cultural identity, as we saw in the previous chapter, is a discursive space of mediation and play for a complex variety of identifications and social relations. The differences that he imagined and noted between himself and the rest of his family, as well as other Black students in the school (as we will see below) are Derridian "differances," retaining elements of what Trevor considers himself different from. He shared a particular cultural identity with both his mother and his four brothers even as he recognized that his place of birth, schooling, and social relationships make him different from them.

Trevor described his mother as having a passion for a whole range of music, from the reggae of the sixties and seventies to the contemporary dance hall varieties that students at Maple Heights talk about. In contrast Trevor told me somewhat cautiously that his music was "the kind you get in clubs." I was unsure what kinds of clubs he was referring to and asked him to explain. He described them as "White, so to speak," and explained that this was because the majority at these clubs are White, "so [the club] would be considered White."

No doubt not wanting to be rigidly categorized and realizing his implication in a racialized discourse, Trevor hastened to add that he attended the clubs for the music and atmosphere, "not just to associate with my own kind." When I returned to the question of reggae music Trevor seemed somewhat defensive: "Oh, I like it too! Actually I like it a lot. They [the White clubs] play it a lot. But not too much." The contradictory claims that are being made here can be understood in relation to the dominant texts of Black identity, and the ways musical tastes and preferences are racialized at Maple Heights. Music and fashion, as we have seen, are signifiers and metaphors for race, but Trevor is resistant to the ways that these associations and metaphors work. As he "cut'n mixes" his musical tastes and the clubs he decides to frequent, he is also aware of how his desires and preferences can be read by others. Having spoken about the choices he was currently making and how those both differed and complemented the choices of his mother and brothers, he took a deep breath and explained, "Well, I don't know." He took another deep breath and continued:

> Like some of these characters I see in the school, like the way they dress. [pause] I'm not, well, I don't want to be perceived that way. Like you see them walking around. They have a certain walk, certain clothes. If you say the wrong thing they'll turn round and start arguing. I don't like to categorize myself. There are days when I feel like, "normal"—whatever "normal" is. I don't categorize myself in a way that I have to wear this, this, or this or else I'm not Black. I don't know. Some of them want to be so pro-Black. Like they will only date Black girls. I find I don't. There is nothing wrong with dating Black girls but there is nothing wrong with dating White people either. So I can go both ways. But for some this is not accepted, so I guess I would not be Black in that sense.

Trevor's distinction between "Black" and "normal" is an interesting example of how Dubois's *double consciousness* works.[5] Dubois draws our attention to how Black people may adopt a double consciousness in the sense of living their lives, or adopting a specific consciousness, in terms of how they are perceived by others. But Trevor's case also calls attention to how such survival strategies for some are also resented. He resents the pressure to be "Black" in his dress and music and denied opportunities to "be normal," or "whatever normal is." He related a story of how, at his previous school, he was told that a "White" student was in fact blacker than he was: "I guess they had this idea that if you're Black then you dress a certain way and you go out with Black people. I couldn't see the logic in that." He continued, "I just want to be a regular guy with my own mind. I want to be seen as Trevor, not just Black." Despite Trevor's desire to be seen as "not just Black," he is also equally aware that this is not always possible because regardless of how he desires his body to be read, he also spoke about how he had been stopped many times by the police as well as approached by individuals, both Black and White, asking him for illegal drugs. He attributes these practices to what Fanon calls "the fact of Blackness."[6]

Trevor's observations demonstrate how race moves back and forth between being a social relation and being an essentialist concept or a positivity. As a social relation race is invoked by the discourse of who Trevor associates with and who he chooses to date. As positivity race is about music, a site of fashion, a certain walk, and perhaps more significantly, the stereotypes that become attached to Trevor's body that result in his being stopped and harassed. These transformations and slippages complicate the meaning of race with the result that Trevor fails to "see the logic," particularly when a White student can be seen as "more Black" than him.

My conversation with Trevor was wide ranging. We

touched on the subject of high school dropouts, a phenomenon that complicates further the discourses of race. He noted that the three students who had dropped out of his OAC economics class were not Black, though one was Guyanese and the other Spanish. I wondered aloud whether Guyanese were not Black. "Guyanese," he explained, "are not Black. We eat the same food but it is the way they speak. They are dark but not really Black." Then what about other students of color, notably those from Ethiopia and Somalia, who attended Maple Heights? How might they fit into this idea of Black? Trevor replied:

I don't really consider them Black either. Seriously. I see a lot of them can speak Italian. They can speak a lot of languages. They're, like, dark on the outside but I guess we're all distinguishable. If I see a Guyanese person and a guy from Somalia I wouldn't say they're Black. I'd say, "He is from Guyana. He is from Somalia." I don't consider everyone to be Black.

"So what is Black?" I asked. He continued:

For me, I see Black as being Jamaican. From . . . [pause] er, not so much from the Caribbean, but Jamaica. People from Jamaica I would say are Black or from Barbados. Well they're *black* Black. Well I guess I'd consider them Black. I guess it depends where they're from that I will consider them Black.

And how about Canadians who are Black and whose ancestors go back many generations? Trevor replied:

Well, I would consider them Black but most Black people wouldn't because they're Black but they are also Canadian. Because they are Black by skin but I guess they wouldn't consider them Black by culture.

Trevor was here eloquently articulating the complexities and contradictions in the meanings of race at Maple Heights. African students from Ghana, for example, spoke about "those Black guys" as they pointed to a group of male students of the Caribbean diaspora occupying a different table and playing dominoes in the school cafeteria. Conversely, Caribbean students identify African students as distinct from Black students. But my question to Trevor, "So what is Black?" may have been unfair because Trevor ended up falling back on the same structures and discourses he critiqued as cumbersome and constraining.

Gio

A few weeks after this discussion with Trevor I had an extended conversation with Gio. Eighteen-year-old Gio is the son of immigrants who came from southern Italy in the seventies. Our conversation began on the subject of tastes in music, which soon led to how he spent his leisure time and where he went "clubbing." One of his favorite nightclubs is one that he described as "Black and Spanish" on Friday nights and "mostly Italians" on Saturdays. On Saturdays he feels "more at home," while he is less comfortable on the evenings when the club is "all mixed up." But Gio talked about going to warehouse parties in downtown Toronto where the parties are also "all mixed up" because "down there the different nationalities know how to have a good time." In the downtown area, it seems, he is able to have a good time because "everything is all mixed up" while in the suburbs being "mixed up" makes him uneasy. But there is another club, "more like a bar," in a different area of Toronto, where Gio had "a mind-blowing experience" one evening. He explained:

> I went into this bar and I saw a whole lot of Black people. That's all I saw, right? Black people—because

of the color of the skin. Then it totally blew my mind. I walked up to the counter and I listened and I thought, "They're all speaking Italian." I don't know where they're from but they were all speaking Italian, because, like in Italy there are a lot of Black people.

Gio was clearly taken aback by this social encounter. Asked about what this encounter did for his understanding of race and specifically the meaning of "Black," he replied, "It just shows that you can't always look at the color of the skin. You have to go deeper into it."

Gio was forced to dig deeper because if we think about race as discursive and about the ways that discourses become embodied, race is not always just about what one sees. The group of Black people, possibly Somalians or Eritreans, speaking Italian unsettles Gio's perceptions of Blackness as a monolithic category. Equally significant though is how the incident may have also been "mind-blowing" to his own sense of identity as Italian. If we think of his identity as intimately invested in the Italian language as a White language, then the incident calls into question one of the foundations on which his identity as White is built. On entering the bar the people that he sees are perceived as the racialized Other. However, not only can they be engaged in conversation, but they can also tell him about places in Rome and in other parts of Italy that he has never seen himself. While they are a curiosity, they are also normalized racially, albeit momentarily.

If we juxtapose the stories and experiences of Trevor and Gio in this chapter with the claims and counterclaims to identity, race, and culture made by other students in the previous chapter, we may note again how the meaning of race is specific to particular times and places. Race is created and recreated within a network of conflicting discourses and converging social relations. It is made intelligible as these youth appeal to culture, community, and notions of belonging and otherness, but the boundaries that they invoke are contextual, arbitrary, partial, and frequently contradictory. What will become clear in my conversations with Margaret and Jane below is that race is also about moral choices and political strategies. Both students are also interesting because they bring the politics of race and the politics of gender to bear upon each other.

Margaret

Margaret, like Trevor, was in her final year of high school and also came to Maple Heights from another local high school. She claimed to be "more at home" at Maple Heights because "there is a lot of intimacy" in contrast to her previous school. She went on to explain that the many Black people at Maple Heights made her "feel more comfortable." But, she explained, "I'm not saying that I am going to get along with everyone but there is more of myself here. And so when I interact with them I am not only interacting with other people but also with myself." Here Margaret imagines a community of race in which her fellow racialized subjects are reflections of herself and vice versa. Within the same conversation, however, this sense of belonging soon gave way to ambivalence.

Margaret was at this stage in the school year a leading member of a group known as the African Queens. (This school organization is discussed further in chapter 5.) Margaret's sense of belonging coupled with her commitment to antiracism and antisexism inspired her involvement in the formation of the group. Margaret lived in an area of Toronto which is known for its concentration of Caribbean people. The area is distinguished by its ethnic difference, seen in the stalls carrying tropical fruits and vegetables, barrels used for shipping goods to the islands, and music hailing from the stores that proclaims roots and hip-hop. But, as I have noted elsewhere, while for some youth this is the place to "feel at home," such feelings may also be fraught with ambivalence.[7]

Margaret's father was born in Jamaica, raised in Trinidad, and now lives in Toronto. Her mother she described as a Jamaican and "prejudiced towards Jamaicans." Despite these origins, Margaret claimed that she was brought up "very Canadian, you can say." She continued, "I think that culture is confusing because if I was looking for an identity, what would it be? I listen to hip-hop. I'm second generation. I don't know a whole lot about Jamaican culture because I have only been there twice." Here Margaret appeared to celebrate the complexity of diaspora and recognize the limits of looking toward roots for identity. Yet at the same time she thought it "important to find identity," as in "this is what Black people wear, this is what Black people listen to." But she also explained the limits to such practices: "It is easy to sit back and be secure knowing 'Ok, I listen to this music. I walk this way, therefore I am.' But I don't think it is viable because hip-hop culture changes so much, like the weather. So even for a small period of time they have an identity, but that changes and then they have to start from scratch."

In her analysis of race, culture, and identity, Margaret was acutely aware of how elusive these categories may be from both her own experience and what she observes. But while she recognized just how fluid these categories may become and recognized the limits of the discourse of roots and identity, she also longed for these categories as stable and capable of being reclaimed. Margaret went on to claim that many members of the Caribbean community have been "so detached from Africa, from our culture, that we have adopted every culture in order to survive. We are all mixed up inside about who we are." Essentialist notions of culture, race, and identity are suddenly invoked. Whereas earlier the limits of essentialism were celebrated, now being "all mixed up" is lamented—even though it is the capacity to adopt that has made for the survival of what can now be recognized as a culture. In these complex and shifting positions, two discourses are competing: the discourse of "roots" and its appeal to fixed origins, and the discourse of "routes," which acknowledges transformations and challenges the integrity of beliefs in the purity of culture and race.

While Margaret lived culture as an inscription of hybridity, she was also aware of Afro-centricity, or what Gilroy names "Africanity."[8] Margaret noted, "There is so much more to our entire race than we know. Sometimes I am in awe of who we really are and what our identity is and our culture." Her reference to "who we really are" would seem to point to an essentialist race and culture which have somehow become diluted by what we have become or what we are becoming, recalling the quotation from the UNESCO publication *Voices in a Seashell* in chapter 1. Margaret then declared her interest in celebrating the African American tradition of Kwanza, though she did hasten to point out that she had little knowledge of what this festival was about. Gilroy helps us to understand the contradictory claims to an African identity, as the "radical utopianism of this appeal to a Black essentialist identity" has the effect of transcending "the parochialism of Caribbean memories in favour of a heavily mythologized Africanity that is itself stamped by its origins not in Africa but in a variety of pan-African ideology produced most recently by Black America."[9]

Politically astute, Margaret also deployed race strategically at Maple Heights. She knew how racist practices marginalized specific groups of students, and her efforts with the African Queens were an attempt to do something about this. She was critical of how Black popular culture becomes not only overly racialized but also sexualized: "A lot of Black guys want to be the tag team sitting around and saying, 'woop, there it is,' pointing to young women's behinds and watching them shake. A lot of the media does that to Black men and women." And she continued, "We are supposed to be desensitized to that. But I am very sensitized!" Margaret's claims to race as identity are therefore contingent and strategic. A racial identity is also a moral and political identity. However, Margaret also refused to be restricted and contained by the choices she made. She could embrace the categories of race and culture and throw the categories to the wind at the same time. Margaret explained:

> At one point I thought of myself as a Black person, and that limits me because as a Black person there are things that I am supposed to be. So I had to shed that. I am not just Black. I am a woman, and that limits me as well. We learn that and it is a form of oppression as well because if I think that I am limited then I don't dare risk anything or try to do anything. So bust being Black and bust being a woman. That is a form of oppression because you are limited in those two little notches.

These moments were astounding for me, coming as they did quite early on in my time at Maple Heights. Margaret's reflections on the disciplinary and constraining effects of the discourses of "woman" and of "Black" spoke volumes to the ways by which identities are strategically deployed. She was very aware of how *strategic essentialism*, in claiming identities, can work for the good of herself and her community.[10] However, Margaret refused to be made into a unitary thing or a mere object of the categories with which she works: "If I think that I am limited then I don't dare take risks." Instead, Margaret was forever taking risks and bringing adventure to bear upon the necessity for identity. She risked, for example, the brunt of comment when she publicly embraced her friend, whom she described as one who "looks like a skinhead" because "he is White, shaves his head, and wears tight jeans," but in fact "you couldn't wish for a nicer person."

José

José was born in El Salvador and is fourteen years old. He came to live in Canada at the age of six. His parents are factory workers who want him to get a good education so that he can "make something of himself" in Canada. Because of where he is from, José falls into the category *Spanish* or *Latino*, but at Maple Heights he tended to distance himself from this category. "In a way I don't really get along with them," he told me about the other students with similar origins. He explained:

> You make a simple joke and they go, "Oh, this guy's not funny." You dress a certain way and they go, "Oh, this guy's Black." You do anything that is right for you, and it's wrong for them. So I haven't really gotten close to them.

While he objectified Spanish students in this way, outside of school he is part of the community of Spanish-speaking churchgoers: "They're not going to stop me from praising my Lord." Then, having talked about how he distanced himself, he added that they are still his friends.

There were several reasons for José's ambivalence toward fellow Spanish-speaking students at Maple Heights, not the least of which was the way this section of the school community is made deviant and singled out as responsible for school fights. (I am aware of only one such fight taking place in the year that I spent at Maple Heights.) But much of the distancing was also due to his own ambivalence around race, complicated by the ways by which sports can be racialized at Maple Heights. José's great passion is basketball and his hero is the superstar Michael Jordan. He told me that he was often called "Baby Jordan," a name in which he took great delight. Indeed, José took delight in any naming which affirmed his particular sense of masculinity, racialized or otherwise, which meant that "they can call me 'stud' or anything else but they must never call me 'faggot.'" While he obviously took delight in being able to cross the boundaries of race, happy to be mistaken for Black, he could not tolerate being mistaken as gay. Racial identity in this case is flexible, but the integrity of his particular brand of masculinity must be kept intact. However, this identification with basketball and being called "Baby Jordan" placed him out on a limb with respect to his Spanish identity:

> The Spanish guys would look at me and say, "Look, this guy's a Black wanna-be," because of the way I dress. I play basketball and I hang around with Black people. I listen to rap music. They call it Black music but I don't because if it was Black music, then I wouldn't be listening to it. It's stuff like that.

José had earlier indicated that he actually took some delight in being mistakenly viewed as Black. But in these last remarks he prefers to be seen as "just Black" and not one who is Spanish wanting to be Black. He knows that rap music is thought of as Black music and therefore his identification with this genre of music might make him Black, but since he knows that he is not Black, he then wonders how the music that he claims as his own can be labeled "Black music." José is able to live with these contradictions of popular culture and race. However, he did not seem willing to allow others to live with similar contradictions in quite the same way, and here gender seemed to be a factor. José explained:

> There was this girl that use to call me a wanna-be. Then she would go to the radio and listen to all this reggae and all this African stuff, and yet she doesn't know anything about Africa. So I said, "No. She's the wanna-be because she doesn't know anything about

Africa and she is listening to that kind of music and stuff because her friends do!"

It is alright for José to embrace rap music without having to prove his knowledge of its social context, and yet his female counterpart's interest in reggae is lumped together with "all this African stuff" and is made invalid on the grounds that she doesn't know anything about Africa. I asked José if this person was also Spanish, to which he promptly replied, "Yeah," and with a laugh he continued:

> And she dress, like. . . . Have you seen those clothes that say "together for ever" with Black people on it and stuff, like the Nubian Sisters? I don't wear that stuff because I'm not Black. And if I see two Spanish or White girls wearing it I feel sorry for them because they're not Black. They can't be Nubian sisters for some reason. I don't know why.

I called José on his double standards: "You wouldn't wear the Nubian Sisters because you're not Black and because you're not female. But you said a few minutes ago that you 'dress Black'?" José replied, "Yeah. Not in the sense of totally Black. I just dress the way I feel comfortable, with baggy clothes because I feel comfortable. I just wear loose clothes." Dressing "Black" was now rearticulated as a matter of comfort rather than a matter of race.

José's distinction between what he calls "normal Spanish" and "Latino" added another dimension to his dress code theories. A Latino look is to wear things like a bandana around the head and a shirt buttoned only at the neck and left untucked. José was not able to describe a female Latino look. As a "normal Spanish" he did not dress the Latino way because his dad "would kill him"; in the dad's words, "It looks crazy." But even as José described himself as "normal Spanish" as distinct from Latino, he returned to how "normal Spanish" may also be mistaken for Black: "I guess if you see me in the street and I pass some guys they'll say, 'That's not a Latino. That's a Black guy,' because I don't dress in the way they do."

The shifts in José's discourse on race and identity are obviously tied to shifts and trends in popular culture, particularly music and dress. This congruence emerged as a very common theme among the youth at Maple Heights. In José's dialogical engagement with race the categories *Latino*, *Spanish*, and *Black* become fragmented and identifications are made with the various fragments in contradictory ways. He hinged together race and culture in such notions as "Black music," but then questioned this racialized designation because of his "normal Spanish" affinity with the music. José's shifting discourses of race and identity are also underpinned by masculinist double standards. He takes pleasure in being mistaken for Black, but he feels sorry for the Spanish and White female students who might want to be equally transgressive in their dress and music because "they're not Black" and therefore cannot be "Nubian sisters" in quite the same way that he is able to be a "Black brother." Then these double and gendered standards are concealed as he attempts to deracialize his own dress by designating it as simply "comfortable."

In these constantly shifting engagements with discourses of race and identity there is also irony and satire. José told me about an incident that had occurred the day before our more extended conversation:

> There was this guy who hangs around with the Spanish people and he's White. He told me, "You still hanging around with those Black guys?" and I go, "Yeah." He says "You can't trust them, man. You got to hang around with your brothers, the Spanish guys." I say "No. You guys racist," And I was afraid he was going to call the Spanish guys and say, "This guy's calling us racist."

Just to be sure I asked José if he had described the person in question as "White." He was ironic in his response: "Yeah. And I was about to say, 'So why don't you hang around with your brothers!'"

Jane

The last case I want to consider in this chapter was an anomaly at Maple Heights for three reasons. Jane identified herself as a White supremacist and a sympathizer of the Heritage Front. Although racism manifested itself in many different forms among youth at Maple Heights, I believe Jane's overtly racist identity and her political affiliations were an anomaly at the school. She was also an anomaly because unlike the other students, who all identify the cultural mix at Maple Heights as its attractive feature, Jane regretted having to pursue her education "in a school with other races and cultures." Third, Jane had no sense of belonging to Maple Heights because her only significant contact was a member of staff "who understands the situation." She was very much a loner at the school. When not in class or standing alone and smoking outside the school, she was reading in the library. She was an avid reader of science fiction, fantasy, history, and anything else she could lay her hands on, "except the romance crap." Despite this last claim, Jane clung to a romanticized notion of history as racially "uncontaminated." If Jane was an anomaly, why include her stories and experiences in this ethnography? Part of the answer to this question has to do with my focus on the discourses that circulate at Maple Heights. This interest is not about quantifying discourses and generalizing on the basis of numbers, but rather about thinking through the relationships between the content and structure of discourses.

Jane was eighteen years old with immigrant parents from Holland and Germany. These ethnic identifications were conflated with the category *Viking* to invoke the fantasy of a pure racial type with which Jane identified. My first contact with Jane was in the same class in which I met the two students whose story opens this chapter. When we talked about the kinds of music that students were listening to, she declared her interest in Oi music, a form of heavy rock that is associated with skinhead culture. Skinhead culture, she explained, had undergone a split with the creation of "Skin Heads Against Racial Prejudice" (SHARP) and its stand against racism. The other faction, with which she identified, is proud of its racism. She castigated SHARP for "bad-mouthing" the faction to which she belongs.

Jane claimed that there are "a lot of good points to being racist." Concealing my disbelief, I asked her about these. In her explanation she drew upon fragments of the familiar discourse which blames multiculturalism for all the perceived social ills of these times. She explained, "I mean, there is a lot of racial tension in the school but no one will talk about it. There is tension in the downtown corridor. And there is a resurgence of everyone looking to their roots." While in her explanation she identified multiculturalism and the search for roots as the problem, it is this problem that legitimizes her affiliations and makes her own identity intelligible. "The problem" seems to ask Jane to celebrate and assert her White identity and, perhaps more significantly, enables her to constitute this identity as being under attack and therefore in need of organizing in order to fight for its rights. Symptomatic of what Balibar calls "neoracism,"[11] the racist discourse that Jane embraced draws upon the progressive language of cultural relativism, which recognizes cultural differences and the need to address inequalities and systematic injustices. She borrows the progressive language but uses it for racist ends. Put another way, neoracism cages racist discourses and practices in politically sensitive language by appropriating the language of oppression for oneself. And as noted in chapter 1, in these practices, race is recoded in the language of culture and identity.

If we recall from chapter 2 the talk and the discourse it subsumes regarding how "everything has now gone too far," of how the dominant culture is under siege from the invading minorities, we might note that while the content of Jane's discourse and the strategies she advocates might be different from others at Maple Heights, they draw on a structure that is familiar to the talk that characterizes the discursive space of schooling at Maple Heights. She claims:

> Nobody is now happy with multiculturalism. The Blacks are frustrated that they have been suppressed for so long and that their heritage is not being taught in school, but if you look, nobody's heritage is being taught. Nobody talks about the Dutch heritage. I have never been taught about the Dutch or even Fleming or Viking. If I was to say I am proud to be White they will say, "Oh, you're racist." Well maybe I am not. I am proud of my background and if that is racist, well, yeah, I am racist. And you can't do certain things any more because you are abusing this person's culture and rights and this and this. I think it is so fanatical now that everyone is losing out.

Jane denied that there was any fanaticism in her own position or in that of the group with which she identified. Instead, her analysis is constituted as objective common sense and in the process negates the distinctions between explanation and evaluation. Jane contrasted the "more complicated" times in which she lives with her imaginary Viking heritage, a time when things were "more Black and White." Consequently she did not like these times because "this is a very depressing state for our country and the world." Jane cited "the immigration problem" as evidence of the depressing state of the world: "We are letting in two hundred and fifty thousand [immigrants]." But then she hastened to add that she did not have anything against immigrants "as such" because, after all, her family were originally immigrants. The problem, however, was that those that are being "let in" are unskilled, mostly unable to speak English, and are people who simply "milk the system." I was not sure if Jane's immigrant parents arrived in Canada from Holland and Germany speaking English, though this is not important. She singled out Somalian immigrants as evidence to support her case. This is a group that she "knows from experience" because they are "always in the coffee shop" down the road from where she lives. So bad is their English, claimed Jane, that they can say "coffee" but cannot say what they want in it. She seemed oblivious to the absurdity of her observations, but we might note that Jane's claims were made at a time when the Somalian community had been turned into an object of study by a Canadian Broadcasting Corporation documentary and was being made racially deviant by the popular press in Toronto.

Jane rightly observed that nowadays, especially with respect to matters of race, "things are more complicated." The stories and encounters that have been cited in this chapter confirm her observations. Race is no longer exactly what it used to be. As Jane held onto a discourse of racial purity on which she based her moral and political choices, all around her she noted the categories fragmenting, transmuting, and contradicting. However, her beliefs in the integrity of purity and racial stability set up the framework by which she is able to engage her Others at Maple Heights. She regrets not being able to attend a school that caters to her race and culture as she put it above. However, at Maple Heights she claims to be able to engage "the guys wearing the fist and the Malcolm X signs on their T-shirts," whom she reads as her Black opposites. She explained, "I understand that and I tell them, 'It's better for you.'" What this means is that nationalist discourses, be they Black or White, as well as what Gilroy calls "ethnic absolutism," provide the logic through which those she perceives as her opposites can be engaged.[12]

Black power for Jane becomes the Other whom she knows from the place of White power where she stands. This is the sense by which the self becomes inscribed in the gaze of the other.[13] Jane clings to certainty in her assertions. However, cracks do appear even in Jane's discourse of racial purity, especially when the issue of religion and European nationalities are talked about. "It's really complicated," she told me. "There are the real purists who say only this part of Italy is White and the other part is interbred with Blacks and others. Greeks are considered White, but some people don't consider them so." Jewish people, she explained, cannot belong because they are seen not as a religion but as a different race. Then within Christianity there are complications because, she told me, there are those who are "Christian identity" and those who are "regular Christians." The former believe that Jesus was Jewish while the latter believe that he was not. Despite these internal differences, however, members of her White group share in common their opposition to what she terms "interracial mixing" because they will say, "Race is my religion."

Racial Identities

The themes that emerge from the various conversations with these youth at Maple Heights are varied, often contradictory, and complex. The youths' identity claims, particularly with respect to race, go in multiple directions. These youth are aware of the representations and the stereotypes through which their various cultural identities are made or are expected to be made, and nearly always refuse to be seen as the passive objects of imagined racial and cultural identities. This means that the making of racial identities is a two-directional process: In the process of claiming who one is, one is also announcing who one is not. Ambivalence is quite central to these processes in all of the cases above, perhaps with the exception of Jane, who insists on greater certainty (though unsustainable) about the meaning of race. Consequently the tensions that we noted with respect to the play of similitude and difference in the last chapter are equally pertinent to the ways that discourses of race inform the work of identity. These youth are racialized subjects, but they situate themselves in the discourses of race in complex and contradictory ways as they both affirm and undermine the racialized constructions of their identities. Youth identify with specific racial formations in their quest for identity, but at the same time they assert their desire to be recognized as different and as bearers of their own beliefs.[14]

In my representations of my conversations we might also note that talk of race and identity is also talk about location, social relations, and popular culture. Talk of race is talk of group identity and of oppression, but it is also talk of fashions, dress, and tastes in music. Racial identifications are also grounded in the other social contradictions that youth live and in the conflicting discourses that circulate at Maple Heights, as we noted in previous chapters. For example, they are grounded in the contradictory discourses of immigrants, class, and nation and the attendant questions of who can belong and who is made Other. Race, as these conversations suggest, is rarely articulated as an isolated discourse, and racial identities are made heterogeneous rather than monolithic. They emerge as unstable and contested and this undermines the static and binary constructions upon which multicultural and antiracist discourses are often premised.

Talk of race is never just about race. I called attention in chapter 1 to how the meaning of race as phenotype and genetic difference, which gave rise to the notion of scientific racism, has long been acknowledged as groundless. I also noted how beliefs in fixed biological differences have given way to beliefs in race as fixed cultural difference, with the effect of producing a "new racism." This, ironically, signals a return to original understandings of race that preceded the ascendency of science in the eighteenth and nineteenth centuries.[15] In the talk of race and racism in this chapter, biology and culture converge when culture is attached to bodies in students' talk about what they see. However, against the backdrop of globalization and migration, of cultural hybridity and creolization, these conversations about race also suggest something about the transitional context in which these youth find themselves. This is a context that is fraught with complexity and contradictions because conventional racist practices and old ways of thinking about race coexist with the new signifiers of race which these youth are in the process of producing.

There are obvious structural constraints that youth encounter because race, like culture, is not made in a vacuum. Trevor, for example, is all too aware of how these constraints work upon him in the forms of harassment he encounters as a Black male, and Margaret is also well aware of how race is complicated by gender. But, while the ascriptions of racial identity work upon these youth in determining ways, what is also striking is the ways that youth work upon those ascriptions. They insist on being active agents rather than simply victims. In the next chapter I draw attention more explicitly to how these processes are further complicated by questions of gender.

5

Gendering Race and
Racializing Gender

The conversations that I drew upon in the previous chapter, except for the one with the two students who had returned to Maple Heights to complete their education, were all one-on-one conversations. In these discussions race and identity emerge as fragmented discourses that shift and slide with context and time. How such categories as *White, Black, African, Spanish,* and *Italian* as well as the notion of different cultures are imagined by youth at Maple Heights is complex and contradictory because these imagined cultures are always lived elusively and ambivalently. How students construct and make sense of these categories is nearly always different from multiculturalism's understanding of different cultures as discrete entities. This means that identities and the cultures of multiculturalism rarely map neatly onto each other. The same, we have noted, is true of discourses of race.

In this chapter, I make a twofold shift in focus. First I want to extend the engagement with private one-on-one conversations by focusing on a public discussion of what students termed "interracial dating." This lunchtime forum was organized by a group named the African Queens, consisting of ten female students. Except for one, all members were Black. The lunchtime discussion was opened to the rest of the school. I pay special attention to this event as a context for the staging and contesting of public discourses of race and gender. In this context both race and gender are presented as fixed social relations. Race is argued for as a set of rules for determining dating arrangements, but as we shall see there is no guarantee that these rules and the disciplining strategies they invoke will be taken seriously. This chapter also pays special attention to how discourses of race become entangled with discourses of gender and sexuality. This process has been evident in previous chapters, but here I make more explicit situations wherein cultural practices are simultaneously gendered and racialized. We will note, for example, how particular students are objectified and sexualized in specific ways, but also how at the same time, these practices are challenged and undermined.

The African Queens

The African Queens had their origins in a dance performance developed by a group of Black female students for African History Month the year before I arrived at Maple Heights. The success of this event, put on at the local community center, led one of its leading members to suggest that they constitute themselves as a social group within Maple Heights for the purpose of consciousness-raising and mutual support around issues related to race and gender. Thus, the formation of the African Queens was an antiracist and antisexist initiative. For the first few weeks of my time at Maple Heights there was considerable enthusiasm among its members for the goals that the group set itself. They came together at lunchtime meetings to talk about their school work and there was evidence that academic performance was improving as a result of the group's mutual help and peer pressure. In keeping with the agenda of consciousness-raising, the Queens also came together for sessions where they wrote and read poetry and stories. These works were generally dedicated to themes of cultural identity and Black pride. The enthusiasm, however, was short lived and internal disagreements and divisions produced tensions and fragmentation. One member described these developments as the result of "too much attitude." Before the end of the first semester few people turned up for meetings, and internal disagreements and terminated friendships replaced the mutual support. By the start of the new semester the organization was forgotten.

The history of the African Queens should not be seen as particularly unusual because many such high school groups evolve and dissolve within short periods of time. However, the demise of this particular group also had something to do with the meaning of culture, race, and identity that it embraced. The discourse of a culture of African Queens, and its subtext of positive role modeling, enabled the group to articulate what they were about in relation to what they opposed. Their sense of difference from other groups at Maple Heights made identity, recognition, and solidarity possible. However, difference within the Queens' ranks appeared to disrupt the sense of cohesion and solidarity invoked by the discourse of difference between. As mapped in chapter 1, difference disrupts similitude. While the Queens publicly argued for race as a set of social relations which regulate relationships, such authoritative discourses of race and identity are contradicted by internally persuasive discourses and the complex and contradictory ways by which identity and race are lived. What follows explores a conflict between public and private discourses of interracial relationships, first in one-on-one conversations with students who were African Queens, and then in the public forum.

Private Spaces

I had several conversations with a student named Tesa, an African Queen who played a leading part in the lunchtime discussion on interracial dating. Tesa is no stranger to controversy at Maple Heights and was singled out by other Queens more than once as "having attitude." She was enrolled in a special program for students who perceived themselves or were perceived by teachers as being at risk of dropping out of high school. She was frequently in the cafeteria when she should have been in class. A number of our conversations took place when she was skipping class.

Tesa seemed to take delight in defying others, including fellow Queens. She was daring, for example, in her embraces of Mark, her roots-identified boyfriend, and was equally daring in the way she chose to dress. On one occasion, for example, Tesa's rather revealing outfit (in midwinter) prompted her fellow African Queens to summon a special meeting to talk about appropriate dress because, they argued, some members appeared not to be able to distinguish between dressing for a party and dressing for school. Tesa listened to the concerns of the group, though whether she acted accordingly was another question. Publicly, both Tesa and Mark were seen as keeping to themselves and therefore to the social boundaries of what was talked about at Maple Heights as "Black culture." However, as both Tesa and Mark quietly explained, this public image concealed their ambivalence towards essentialist notions of race and culture. Mark, now in his late teens, is a father and carries a photograph of his son in his wallet. He hastened to tell me that the mother, now his former girlfriend, is White. On another occasion, when a Black student dismissed a fellow Black student for being "so White," Mark quietly said, "Nothing wrong with White people," and turned to tell me that his best friend through junior high school was an Italian boy. Mark took no part in public discussions but in the public forum discussed below, he contributed to the chorus of cheers, boos, and jeers that erupted in the back of the class-room.

Two weeks before the African Queens' lunchtime meet-ing on interracial dating I met Tesa in the cafeteria. I was at the time engaged in conversation with two other students, a male from Ghana and a female from Ethiopia. Tesa was sit-ting at the adjacent table but from this position insisted on contributing to the conversation that we were having. The conversation started when the Ghanian student suddenly asked me for my thoughts on the subject of interracial rela-tionships. I threw the question back to him, and he replied, "Love knows no color." Overhearing this, Tesa intervened from the other table about the importance of "sticking to your own kind" for "better understanding." When the two students left for their classes Tesa stayed behind and moved to my table in order to make the case that "people's cultures are different" and therefore they should date within their own culture and race. To cross the boundaries of race was to invite trouble and misunderstanding, she insisted. Culture is here imagined as acting upon people and setting the terms for who can belong and who cannot. But Tesa then revealed another side of the story. Her position was entangled with personal experiences and conflicting desires, as well as the complications and implications of history and the politics of race.

Tesa had been involved in a special relationship for some time with "a White guy" who was "very good" because he was "a caring guy." She felt her family did not like the idea of her "dating outside the race and culture." Moreover, she was uncomfortable and unsure how the boyfriend's family felt about the relationship. She discussed her anxiety about being treated simply as a racialized object, a feeling difficult to explain because other than the attitude of her family, she was unable to find any evidence to support it. But after a brief but pregnant break in our conversation, Tesa continued, "You know, things can happen because there can be problems in relationships." She went on to explain that "everyone had problems." The problem, however, seemed to be the question of how her particular relationship might be racialized. "Well, your man might slap you around the ears. I mean that happens. But, you know if a White guy raises his hand to me . . ." After a deep breath she continued, "Well it's like slavery all over again."

This moment seemed to speak volumes about the legacy of slavery and the burdens of culture, race, and identity. I was struck by a sense of the individual as the bearer of history. Also stunning was the distinction that Tesa made between "your man" and "their man" or the "Other man." Given her earlier position on "sticking to your own kind," I read her distinction as being between Black and White. She appeared to suggest that sexism and male chauvinism on the part of "her man" could be understood and rationalized, if not condoned or encouraged. Similar actions on the part of "a White guy," on the other hand, are read quite differently. His actions are not simply individual acts of abuse and male chauvinism, but are also read as the embodiment of a long history of racial oppression and racialized violence. They become a racialized act of chauvinism. Again, if we recall here how the male White student in the last chapter who identified as "normal Canadian" racialized the actions of the Black female who obstructed his path, we might note the same structures and process of racialization. In the moment of normalizing certain kinds of masculinist behavior, the notion of racial deviancy (which I introduced in the last chapter) is turned on its head: while the "normal Canadian" (White Canadian) marks the Black female student as racially deviant, for Tesa the acts of Black masculinity and chauvinism are made racially normal, albeit momentarily, and the actions of a White male are made deviant. Such complexities, however, are repressed by Tesa in public spaces. Her previous affair with the White male is a private matter, unlike her current relationship with Mark.

Racialized discourses of dating are further complicated by what is referred to as "shadism," or preference for light-ness in skin tone in the tradition of the "pigmentocracy" that prevailed in the colonial and now postcolonial Caribbean context.[1] Both Tesa and Mark are well aware of this history but Tesa suggests that Mark is its greater victim, since "his family treat him bad because he is the darkest," and she wonders whether his fathering a child with a White girl-friend is the result of this treatment. In this case, Mark's choices are seen as the result of history rather than choice or desire. Significantly, Tesa privately acknowledges the conflicts in her desires as well as the ambivalence that they produce, but as she attempts to lead a public discussion on interracial relations, she asserts the determining effects of history. In so doing, the ambivalence that marks her private thoughts and actions is concealed by the certainty that marks her performance in the public space.

Public Spaces: The Forum on Interracial Dating

The crowding and constant movement of people made it difficult to count the number of students who filled the class-room for the African Queens' special lunchtime discussion on interracial dating, but there seemed to be approximately sixty students present. All grade levels appeared to be represented, though the majority of students I knew were from the upper grades of the school. There was a great deal of enthusiasm and excitement and the noise level was quite high. Tesa, who was chairing and facilitating this meeting, eventually brought some order to the room and opened the forum by asking the very general question, "So what do you think of interracial relationships?" The question met a very brief moment of silence and then a male student sitting near to Tesa at the front of the class responded, "Excuse me! That doesn't answer the real question. You know that there is all this fuss from the Black girls when I'm talking to a White girl!"

An outburst of shouts, cheers, and jeers followed this response, but Tesa did not seem at all perturbed. As the disorder subsided, a second male voice interjected, "For me it's a personal choice." Again a chorus erupted as individuals who were unable to have their opinions heard by the larger forum put them to the persons sitting or standing beside them. A female student who insisted on being heard then intervened, and calmly and seriously advised the others present that they should "keep to your own kind" because in that way there is "better understanding." This led to accusations and counteraccusations: "Trouble with Black girls, they got attitude!" shouted a male voice from the back of the class. "But you're the one with the attitude," came the response.

By this point the forum seemed a place to test the field and to provoke reactions from those present. There was also irony and parody. The claim that "Black girls have attitude" was countered by the accusation that Black men treat White women better than they do Black women. Then amid the boos that greeted this response, Tesa asked the men if they thought White women were "easier." During the uproar over the way that "easy" was being racialized, Tesa appeared to be smirking.

Tesa returned to the discourse of race as biology to suggest that contaminating races by mixing was a social and cultural problem. She asked, "What about the children and people that are half-and-half?" The phrase "half-and-half" brought a new intensity to the debate. "Let them speak for themselves. We have some here," came a voice from the back. Students looked in the direction of two embarrassed students standing in the doorway, singled out as "half-and-half" among the crowd who all were, to borrow this discourse, in various ways "halves" and fractions of backgrounds.

Margaret, whom we met in an earlier chapter, rose to her feet clearly angered by this invocation of race as biology. "Excuse me! Excuse me!" she shouted over the voices of the animated students. "What is this 'half-and-half'? What is this way to talk about people—pointing to them as if they are freaks! There are no half-and-halves here. There are only people!" Margaret's intervention was greeted by applause from all sides of the room. Theorizing race as biology was one thing. Identifying individuals as objects of racist discourses was not to be tolerated in this public forum.

The chatter subsided after Margaret's intervention and Tesa returned to her agenda which, it seemed, was to pin down the opinions and positions of the male students present. "How do you feel when you see a Black girl with a White guy?" she asked. A male student sitting at the front of the class responded, "To be honest, it depends on who I'm with at the time. Personally I don't care, but what you say depends on who you are with at the time." There was laughter and Tesa seemed to be under pressure but she persisted: "Can I ask what girls have dated White guys?" There was a range of boos and cheers as people looked around to see whose hand was raised. Some hands were raised boldly and defiantly, others shyly. I noticed that Tesa's hand was not raised in response to her own question. It was also interesting that she did not ask the males present to raise their hands in the same fashion. As people giggled about whose hands were raised, another female student explained aloud that she would not date a White guy because "for a start his parents wouldn't accept it. And this is for real because I know of this girl that it happened to." From the back of the room came the response, "Garbage. You discriminating White people!" For the first time, one of the five White students present clamored to be heard. "Can I say something?" she repeated. Quiet slowly returned and she held forth: "For a start you are all going on and talking about White guys treating Black girls better. But what about the White guys that also treat them badly? And what about White guys who treat White girls badly? You talk about White and Black, but there is good and bad all [a]round." There was loud applause. "That one is good. She talks sense," said a voice from the back.

Many people were now clamoring for the opportunity to say something on this passionate subject. Tesa seemed to be having a good time even though things were out of hand. The school bell rang signaling the end of the lunch period and therefore this forum on interracial dating. There were no other forums on interracial dating, and no others organized by the African Queens. However, this one became the reference point for many conversations with students for the rest of the semester.

I provide this sketch of the lunchtime forum because despite, or perhaps because of its chaos and theater of accusations and counteraccusations, it tells us something about the dynamics of race and culture and the politics of identity in public spaces. Within this space personal desires meet both the humanist claim that "race doesn't matter," and the politics of race and identity. In the previous chapter we observed the shifting signifiers of race. During the forum on interracial dating the students attempt to stabilize the meanings of race in order to mark and police the boundaries of dating. The very concept of *interracial* is dependent on a discourse of races as fixed and separate entities. But the chorus of cheers and jeers that both applaud and mock monolithic racial categories, as well as strategies for determining who dates whom, demonstrate how stabilizing attempts also fall down within the same space. Under these circumstances race, like culture, becomes elusive.

Discourses of race as a fixed set of social relations made the forum possible and the proceedings intelligible by setting the parameters for what could be thought in the first place. But it is also possible that the forum was called precisely because the fixity of race was falling apart among youth. Such flux was perhaps most obvious in the "half-and-half" debate. One moment the two individuals were identified as different, as "freaks" as the angry student put it, and as such were made Other to Black. They were held up as the troubling consequences of mixing stable biological entities and transgressing racial boundaries. But then Margaret, who in the previous chapter identified herself as Black, angrily asserted that those who are identified as "half-and-halves" or as "freaks" are in fact "just like us." This could mean that they are "individuals" just like us, "Blacks," or if we recall the sentiments of John from the previous chapter, just like us because "even in the mix there is a mix."

From the onset of this public forum the stakes were suspect. A seemingly innocent question, "What do you think about interracial relationships?" was read as concealing a deeper wish to control the desires and the choices of Black males. The Queens' question was perceived as a coded version of a populist discourse which holds that "our Black brothers are ignoring us." (We can only speculate on what the stakes might have been had there been a group identified as "African Kings" running a similar forum.) This populist discourse makes problematic the possibility of leaving the options open or, to return to Derrida, allowing for those situations where chance meets necessity. Specific genders are racialized as "having attitude" when the attitudes of some are constituted as the attributes of the racial group. Black males are accused of treating women of the other race better than they treat their own. Gender and personal relationships are in these ways racialized, but race is also gendered because how one reacts depends on the gender of the other race.

Another related process in these conflicting discourses is the racializing and gendering of sexual identities. Sexual "easiness" is racialized in the question of which race is "easier," then gendered because it is attached only to women. Consequently, these discussions reproduce females as sexual objects. This discourse is reproduced by both men and women in the accusations and counteraccusations regarding "easiness." The double standard was never in question during this discussion but instead further legitimized by the argument that both races have "easy" females. Racializing and gendering "easiness" reinstates sexism.

Stereotypes of Black masculinity incorporating what Mercer notes as the codes of machismo and domination are also naturalized in these discussions.[2] These forms of racialized masculinity both facilitate and constrain. The myth of the racialized stud can make for a positive self-image. Here we might recall José from the previous chapter, who takes delight in being mistaken for Black and wants to be called "stud." However, he cannot tolerate being called "gay" because this identity challenges his masculinist ideal. Here, the policing strategies that are at play in the forum on interracial relations overdetermine Black as a category, in contrast to Whiteness which, as Dyer notes, is able to have an everything and nothing quality about it.[3] Whiteness both stands in as the norm and plays itself off as invisible. Black, on the other hand, becomes the signifier of difference, and is policed from the outside and inside. It is denied the range of human subjectivity opened to White. Consequently, the structures of racism are reinstated.

The forum on interracial relations was one of the last functions organized by the African Queens. As I have already indicated, by the end of the semester the group was disintegrating and by the start of the second semester it was defunct. The significance of the aims and aspirations of this group cannot be underestimated. As noted, the formation was a bold initiative and the group's objective of confronting racism and sexism should be seen as part of the larger project of antiracism. The Queens also set as their agenda working for unity and cooperation in the face of what was frequently touted as disunity among "our people." However, from the start of my time at Maple Heights cracks emerged in the call for unity and a sense of cohesion. The group's short history may not be different from that of any other school-based youth group, but it offers significant insights into the limits of the discourse of race, culture, and empowerment around which the group organized itself. Internal arguments about what constituted "Black" and what constituted appropriate Queen behavior demonstrated that there were no guarantees of the stability of the categories of race and gender. Empowerment seemed to be dependent on suppressing difference, that is, not the differences that distinguished the Queens from the rest of the students, but the differences among themselves. It also seemed contingent upon a notion of culture as the attributes that distinguished this group within the school. What it could not tolerate, however, was the Queens' own ambivalence to the terms and rules imposed by this meaning of culture. Furthermore, while the name "African Queens" was meant as a term of empowerment, perhaps it worked against the group because usually there is only room for one queen.

But the concept of elusive culture suggests we also think about the history of this group in terms of opportunities for experimentation and play. While these students embraced the meaning of culture suggested by the metaphor of African royalty (and here we might note shades of the sense of culture and identity, expressed in the UNESCO publication *Voices in a Seashell*, as that which can be recovered), they also played with it and refused to allow it to constrain them. Membership in the African Queens was an opportunity for experimentation and fun, but rather than be disciplined by this meaning of culture, the students moved on to something else.

Private Space

Several months after the interracial forum, and therefore after the disintegration of the African Queens, I was involved in separate conversations with June, who had been one of the members. Like Tesa, June displayed a passion for dressing up: "We love clothes. We love to dress. We like to make an appearance." She explained that other students in the school also liked to dress up, but while she believed these other groups "just look at each other and say, 'That looks good,'" her former Queens and other friends are also interested in outdoing each other. June then declared that she did not care about what other people thought of her, nor about fitting in. Her actions and other remarks, however, indicated that June was very concerned about fitting in with her peer group and their experiments and competitions with style. She also liked to emulate her favorite singer, Toni Braxton. But "fitting in" was also about standing out and appearing to be different from the others around her. June was well aware of this irony. She also knew that while she reproduced some of the stereotypes of her friends and of the Queens, she mocked those stereotypes at the same time.

June and I revisited the Queens' forum on interracial relations, where she had positioned herself at the front of the crowded classroom and made known in this public space her disapproval of interracial relations on the grounds that they "only cause problems." She was not specific about the nature of these problems. In our private conversation June told me she had been confronted by her friends for the position she had taken at that public meeting. She qualified her position to me by explaining that while interracial relations were fine for other people she did not believe in them for herself. This then shifted as our conversation continued, which may have something to do with her inability to pin down exactly what interracial relations really meant. How, for example, did the Spanish-speaking students who were so frequently targeted as different at Maple Heights fit into the equation? June explained, "There's a lot of times that I would like to communicate with some Spanish guys in this school, but I just don't see myself with them." Before giving me a chance to question her she moved on: "The other day I was talking to this guy and he was 'mixed'." June then stopped momentarily and added, "I don't know what led to this because I like to keep my personal life personal." I was reminded of Tesa, who distinguished between those relationships that are made public and those that are kept private. Breaking with the rule of keeping the personal, personal, June told the story of how she was confronted by a Black male friend of hers at Maple Heights who confused "mixed" and "White." She related the encounter: "He said, 'I hear you're going out with a White guy.' And it was like, 'Ugh. Get away from me!' So I got back at him and said, 'Look, you're Black and I picked a White guy over you.' But I only said that as a joke because I don't see myself doing that right now. Maybe later, but right now I'm just scared of the problems. I think lots of people may be nicer than your own kind but right now I'm scared." The problems to which June referred were explained in terms of a history similar to Tesa's. But another problem, reflected in the story she related, had to do with what others think and with how identities are policed.

If we return to the question of how power works through opposing discourses of race, gender, and sexuality, we might note that power facilitates but also becomes a hindrance or a stumbling block to desires, and therefore is the starting point for an opposing strategy. The strategies that both Tesa and June deployed entailed keeping separate their public and private positions on race and interracial relations. This meant allowing those relationships that conform to group expectations to become public, in part because relationships that are reproduced through racialized discourses as being "with your own kind" are made normal, while those that are read as different are made deviant. But we also see June affronting the codes of machismo and domination, frequently attached to Black sexuality, with her joke about choosing White masculinity over Black. While these codes might go unchallenged in the public space, in private June has her own strategy for opposing them. June, like many of the other youth at Maple Heights, is fully aware that she is performing a particular racialized identity and imagined Blackness in public, even though she claims it as inherent to her community.

June was teased by one of the cheering male students from the back when she raised her hand to indicate that she had dated a White student. Several months later June told me that interracial relationships were the "big thing." She explained, "Right now there are a lot of Black guys going after White girls and lots of White girls going after Black guys." Again the desires and activities of the Black girls remained unspoken. I questioned June on something I had overheard earlier about light skin and what was called a "nice complexion." June laughed. "Have I caught you?" I asked. "Trust me, you have!" she laughed. "With me, I like light skin guys better." June talked about "nice" hair and her desire to have a child with "nice hair and nice complexion." Surprising to me about this moment was how discourses of shadism and hair textures appeared to persist despite the impact of Black cultural politics which champion the natural features of Black beauty and the discussion of Black differences. Here we might note how aesthetic distinctions have always been central to the ways that racism divides the world through binaries and a corresponding judgement of human worth.[4]

June's boyfriend at the time, whom I did not meet, was apparently so light that he was also mistaken as "White." But in addition, June explained, "They call him Paki. They call him all kinds of names that they call a mixed kid." For these reasons, the boyfriend wished that he could change to Black. When I mentioned that I had understood the boyfriend to be Black already, June explained that he is because he likes the music and the dress of Black culture, and that she had meant "more Black." But as we saw in the last chapter, there is no neat correspondence between how one's body is read and how one desires it to be read. Race as culture and race as phenotype are not reducible to each other, which is the cause of the boyfriend's frustration, but at the same time these multiple ways of living in a racialized body work to the advantage of June's pleasures and desires.

In his last film, *Black is Black Ain't: A Personal Journey Through Black Identity*, Marlon Riggs calls attention to how sexuality that departed from the perceived norms of hetero-sexuality and interracial relationships produced consider-able anxiety for nationalist projects.[5] The name "African Queens" itself gestures toward a specific kind of Afrocentric nationalism with assumptions about men as kings. Race, gender, and sexuality are inseparable in this discourse, but its consequences are different for men and women. The public forum, even as it attempts to discipline the males present, in effect reinscribes the practice of punishing women by asking them to raise their hands if they have "crossed the line." Here we might also recall the ways by which Tesa and other female students who expressed the same sentiments carry the bur-den of history in how they imagine their relationships and what becomes acceptable and unacceptable from Black and White men.

Both the public and private spaces that these students occupy and speak from are social spaces, and as these youth take up positions on relationships within them, they do so cognizant of the fact that such spaces are constituted by com-plex and contradictory sets of relationships that both con-strain and enable their desires and the construction of their identities. To understand how culture imposes constraints on the choices, actions, and experiences of these youth we might return to the traditional understanding of culture as attributes, the sentiments of *Voices in a Seashell* in chapter 1. In these talks of interracial relationships, such an under-standing of culture becomes inseparable from an under-standing of race as a fixed set of attributes. This understand-ing of culture and race as a dyad is evoked by both males and females to sanction specific kinds of dating patterns and to make others deviant. As I have noted above, however, these discussions in both the public and private settings take place precisely because this more rigid understanding of race and culture is falling apart and becoming more elusive. The contradictions of race constantly surface. The recourse to the history of slavery as a basis for securing community based on race also produces its own set of tensions: this history is gendered—the slap of the White man. But even as these students invoke this history they simultaneously invoke the contradictions and their desire to transcend the burden of this history.

A view of culture as elusive and fluid, rather than rigid and determining, helps us to understand the multiple strategies and shifting positions that youth take up in these different and conflicting discussions. It also helps us to understand how they live their lives and construct identities in relation, and often in opposition, to the constraints imposed by gender, race, and culture. Consequently, even though race and culture might be argued for publicly as a set of rules for determining dating arrangements, or as providing the blueprint for appropriate race/gender behavior, there is no guarantee that these rules will be respected. And finally, juxtaposing the discourses that are sanctioned in public spaces with the internally persuasive discourses that one encounters in the private space is not by any stretch of the imagination an attempt to legitimatize one over the other. What it does instead is to call attention to how race can be made contingent and to underscore some of the tensions through which it (like culture and identity) is lived.

6

Toward an Understanding
of Elusive Culture

There is a dilemma and a peculiar kind of irony in writing about elusive culture and positing its characteristics. The concept is an attempt to gesture toward a view of culture as an ongoing process attuned to the ambivalent and contradictory processes of everyday life. This is a view of culture as emergent and continually in the making rather than as foreclosed. And yet the very process of writing about it can be seen as an act of foreclosing and fixing what I want to acknowledge as being in continual flux. This is now an established dilemma in ethnographic writing. The ethnographer, as Geertz notes, "inscribes" social discourse, writes it down, and in the process "turns a passing event that exists in its moment of occurrence, into an account which exists in its inscriptions and can be reconsulted."[1] This book offers no way out of the dilemma except to acknowledge my implication in the ethnographic creations. Since I undertook this research, the informants about whom I write have moved on. They now occupy different contexts and circumstances in the world of work and higher education, for example, where new sites of identity, new sets of relationships, and new cul-

123

tural practices present themselves and are juggled with old identifications as identity insists on being, as Hall expresses it, "a process of becoming."[2]

I have returned to Maple Heights since completing the research and have found that the school too has been taking steps to change its official identity. I found that several of the teachers with whom I spoke and who feature in one way or another in this book have moved on, in some cases to retirement and in other cases to new positions in other schools. A striking new feature of Maple Heights is that students now wear school uniforms, which means that the more obvious dress codes that signaled the different identifications with specific youth cultures are no longer evident. There are also new curriculum orientations and other efforts being made to invoke a new and changing sense of identity in the face of what I described in chapter 2 as a "spoiled identity." The changes are an ongoing effort to improve the quality of education and the image of the school to attract students in the face of threats of school closures and government financial cutbacks.

Having acknowledged the dilemma of ethnography arresting the course of events in their normal flow over time, I confirm the sense in which this work is like a series of snapshots of my encounters and conversations and the interpretations that I bring to them. Elusive culture admits to its own sense of time. But what is significant is that time does not change in the ways that the history of Maple Heights is conceptualized. This was borne out over the course of writing this book when I presented parts of it to audiences of graduate students and school teachers alike. What was striking about these presentations is that there was always more than one person present who was convinced that he or she knew the school about which I write. At no time, however, has anyone been right about the actual place at which I undertook this research project. The fact that individuals recognize and in some cases claim to know

Maple Heights is significant for the conceptual framework that I bring to this work. My chief concern throughout the course of the research and the writing of this book has been with trying to identify the available discourses that circulate at any given time. I have been interested in how discourses act upon people, both students and teachers, but also with how individuals rework and act upon discourses in different ways. I have also tried to think about why some discourses, for example discourses of multiculturalism and of how the nation is imagined, are so persistent while others, for example discourses of the popular cultures of youth, might be more fleeting. The tension that is produced as persistent discourses encounter more fleeting ones is a theme to which I want to return below.

As noted in chapter 1, I avoid all pretense of and aspirations to presenting a realist ethnography, modeled on positivist claims to total truth. Ethnography as it is understood here is not the process of recording the attributes of what makes a good or bad school. What makes a good or bad school will always be in dispute. And yet as readers come to recognize the discourses that are present and to know the school through these discourses, the ethnography is clearly evocative of a real place and real people to which readers might relate.[3] This means that Maple Heights might be any school, or it could be many schools. In this sense, while refusing claims to representativeness this ethnography might well provide the basis for reflecting upon the place of schooling in a more general sense.

This brings us back to the concept of a discursive space. The emphasis on discursivity, as I have noted, works against the practice of simply representing the culture as a set of attributes. It pays attention instead to the qualities of discourses that circulate and which open or foreclose the different ways people can imagine themselves and the school. The larger question that this focus on discursivity opens up for researchers and educators alike concerns the conditions that might be created in order to allow people to explore fluidity rather than rigidity.

The notion of a discursive space recognizes that the ethnographic site at which the study of race, culture, identity, and gender is conducted cannot be divorced from the larger social context of the global city wherein the school is located. But discursivity also goes beyond the belief that the site simply reproduces external ideologies and external structures of power. Discursive space recognizes that the school is implicated in unequal relations of power, but by drawing on what Giddens describes as a "duality" of actions and structures and de Certeau's notion of "spacial practices,"[4] my focus on the everyday practices of schooling asks us to think about how the structures that are often conceptualized as merely coming from the outside are in fact present in the everyday actions of groups and individuals. Structures in this sense are the materiality of the ideas and belief systems. As such, structures are also about knowledge—how knowledge is produced and legitimated. In this case, at stake is a knowledge of neighborhoods, historical processes, communities, urban change, how youth are constructed, and so on. One of the questions that this book subsequently raises is how the concepts with which I work—difference, globalization, diaspora, and identity, for example—and the ethnographic details that illustrate them, may expand the parameters of the knowledge which we bring to bear on questions of community, multiculturalism, and antiracism. In chapter 2 we noted that the structures of multiculturalism, racism, and antiracism are sustained by discourses that are continually being reworked in everyday experiences. If we think about structures in this way, individuals are seen not merely as objects of structures but as subjects who are producing and acting upon structures even as they are constrained by them. This observation is cognizant of the larger and unequal economic, social, and political dynamics, but if structures are the materiality of ideas and the workings of discourses, then they are also cultural. It follows that the distinction that is often invoked between structures and cultures by antiracist discourses cannot be sustained.

Conceptualizing schooling as a discursive space enables us to recognize how individuals come from contradictory locations and occupy contradictory positions. This makes it difficult to neatly categorize them in terms of the binaries of good/bad. As we have seen, both teachers and students shift and slide in relation to the policies and practices of antiracism, discourses of multiculturalism, and discourses of identity. They do so even as they make identity discourses their own. The place of ambivalence, of what Bauman describes as living with the tensions of opposing views and positions, is quite central to these processes.[5]

Understanding the school as a discursive space also draws attention to the specificity of racism and how racist subjectivities are formed in one situation and then reconstituted as something different in another. We noted how one might embrace racist sentiments and act in racist ways in one situation, while also demonstrating benevolence and concern for equality in another. It is this capacity to embody multiple subjectivities, to continually reconstitute oneself within different discourses, and to borrow from one in order to nullify the insidious effects of the other that gives racist practices their affectivity. These processes are further complicated as discourses of race and racism are also submerged in concerns with nation, ethnicity, and gender. Recall, for example, how the nation-state of Canada is imagined as kind, caring, and accommodating in contrast to the United States, which is imagined as assertive in its demands for conformity and for "beating its chest." But at the same time, because it is "caring and kind" Canada is also imagined as letting "everything go too far" and "everything" becomes a muddled discourse that subsumes questions of human rights, social welfare, violence, family rights, and even the right to display Christmas trees. Multiculturalism can be invoked as metaphors that conflate all the perceived ills of contemporary society. In these ways discourses of liberal sentiments rub up against popular conservative discourses and subjects may slide ambivalently between the two. One can embrace liberal sentiments and be bothered by them at the same time. These ethnographic observations also confirm the assertion made in chapter 1, that while academic distinctions are made between the concepts culture, race, ethnicity, and identity, the distinctions come undone in everyday discursive practices.

In my elaboration of the concept of elusive culture I have drawn upon the distinctions that are made in other school ethnographies between official and unofficial cultures, or between *culture* and *subculture*.[6] But the notion of elusive culture also departs from those works in which class is the dominant organizing principle. At times class is the significant principle, as in the way that the area around the school is constituted as being "among the poorest in Metro Toronto," as one of the teachers commented. And at Maple Heights there are many other students, like José in chapter 4, whose own desire and that of their parents is to be able to rise above the current social and economic conditions in which they find themselves. But in all cases, and in the ways that social relations are lived at Maple Heights, there are other organizing principles in addition to class. By opening up the question of the discursivity around these other organizing principles such as race, gender, and ethnicity, we see how easily they converge as race may be confused with class, class with gender, and so on. Convergence is evident when the cultural forms and expressions which these youth adopt, such as clothes, language, and musical interests, are deemed to define racial groups but might have nothing to do with phenotype. Recall from chapter 4 Bena, who is read as Black one moment even as he is seen as "*white* White" the next moment, or the case of Trevor, whose body is Black and therefore acted upon in particular ways when he is going about his business and his pleasures around the city, but who is read by some of his fellow youth as more White than many White students. Recall also the case of Marta in chapter 3, who sees herself as Spanish even though she is Serbian. In these everyday constructions and the social relations they suggest, youth can be Spanish, or Black, or White, but they can be so in ways that may have nothing to do with how dominant discourses define Spanish, Black, and White. What this tells us is that these names and the categories they invoke are not literal and fixed identity markers, but sets of relationships. These are relationships between students, but they are also relationships to the representations and representational practices through which identity is imagined. In other words, they are social as well as psychic relationships—relations between individuals and social groups, and at the same time relationships to ideas, fantasies, representations, and discourses as well as affective desires. They are relationships of belonging that may shift with the conflicts of desires and relations shaped by the racist practices stemming from the hardened discourses of race that marginalize, alienate, and brutalize.

By its attempt to engage the fluidity that marks the sets of relationships through which culture, race, and identities are made, this ethnography suggests a departure from works that view the school and the community and the organizing dynamics of race and class as stable spaces and entities. In chapter 2 I offered a glimpse of how class shifts. The ways that urban change occurs and the ways that new groups move in and move out into other areas again is also very much the pattern of class progression in North America. These developments, as we have seen, are all too often constituted as a haunting history and as a problem of neighborhood, rather than as a theory of urban space and urban change. When conceptualization is made rigid in this way it is stripped of any ambivalence, and educators may minimize their own capacity to separate fantasized and imagined history from their own anxieties about the school and the bodies that populate it. Consequently, one imagines school as a place where changing demographics are equated with the rise of crime and the school is suspected merely because of the racial markers that occupy it and are invoked in the telling of its history. There is a gap between two sets of experiences at play in the conceptualization of schooling: those of the students and those of the teachers. These are not necessarily generational gaps, but cultural ones. The things that the teachers are passionate about and are being summoned in talk about what Maple Heights used to be are gone—lost objects. What the students are passionate about, on the other hand, teachers have less access to, and there is little or no knowledge to bridge that gap.

What I am positing here is a different conceptualization of school and community. This is one that sees the city as a site of profound movement and difference to which the school stands in relation. Indeed, it is this sense of movement and difference that makes the school, as well as the school making it. By the beginning of the twenty-first century what are now named "visible minorities" will indeed be the "visible majority" in Toronto, and our theories of dominant and minority culture will have to be revised to reflect and engage these demographics. [7] To understand these developments better, we might return to some of the concepts that are sketched in the first chapter and a series of tensions that are produced by the dynamics to which these concepts refer. In particular I return to the concepts difference, globalization, and diaspora and how they open up questions about culture, race and identity as well as how school knowledge proceeds.

Two questions will shape the discussion that follows. The first might be self-evident: Why study these youths' experiences of race, sex, gender, culture, and identity? The second, based on the observations made in this book, concerns what would actually be at stake for education to think about these various identity markers as social relations and not just attributes. Expressed another way, why study these experiences as experiences, as opposed to stable markers of identity? What does it mean to consider race as an experience, as opposed to a phenotype? Or what does it mean to think about gender as an experience of belonging and longing? The students, as we have seen, live their identities through social relations. They have to defend themselves, as in the group meetings when people are trying to argue for race and sex, or when the African Queens are making the case for the double play of race and gender. They have secrets, desires, and fantasies about race, culture, and identity which are not always consistent and coherent. The passion of identity or the passion for identity means that there are strong feelings about who they admire or how they come to be. They know how to work with the representations, both negative and positive, through which they imagine themselves, but they also know how to discard them or to refuse their disciplinary effects. They live and work with the inconsistencies and contradictions of building youthful identities rather than shatter under their effects. All of this suggests that students are making themselves in relation to others, and identity in this sense is always relational.

Returning to chapter 1 and *Voices in a Seashell*, as we have seen, at some level education does seem to acknowledge the lived experience of students. This is not a problem. However a problem seems to lie in the ways lived experiences are conceptualized in curriculum materials, pedagogical relations, and assumptions about communities. There one might observe a series of rigidities and older anthropological orientations toward an attribute theory of culture premised on the belief that this is how different cultures can be known. Multiculturalist discourses and the desire for inclusiveness produce a theory which suggests that if you have a logic of Others' culture, then you can know how to accommodate them, join them, or stay away from them.

When conceptualization of what it means to know cultures is made rigid in this way it is stripped of ambivalence or questions and yet, as we have seen throughout this book, the ways individuals see themselves in relation to their cultural representations are full of ambivalence, questions, and conflicts. The desire to know cultures, races, and identities as stable objects detracts from the possibility of engaging with the multiple identifications and affiliations which we have seen are central to the ways that identities, race, and culture are made and lived by youth. The culture of schooling is not a steady thing to protect, but something that people are making. It is not simply something that they receive. The youth in this study live the theories of identity in all their complexity. They demonstrate tremendous flexibility in their capacity to experiment, take risks, and create and discard ideas. In this sense there is also resistance to seeing knowledge and identity as something to apply or to force others to have. Knowledge opens possibilities for doubts and ambivalence. Those who hold more rigid ways, for example the student named Jane who insists upon certainty about her knowledge and identity as Aryan Nation and sympathizer with the Heritage Front, seem to have a difficult time compared with those who are continually interrogating the boundaries by which "all the different cultures" (to recall the returning Italian student from chapter 4) as well as the self are imagined. We might consider Jane from chapter 4 in relation to Margaret from chapter 5. Both have an intuitive sense of the importance of history and discourses of race to making identities for themselves, but while Jane insists on a certain rigidity for her claims, Margaret appears more flexible. One moment Margaret claims the identity categories and contingently works with them. The next moment she throws them to the wind. Margaret recognizes and lives with the contradictions of identity. Jane closes down contradictions and conceals the tensions for the sake of asserting certainty.

If schooling is orientated only toward self-esteem and the celebration of folk culture, then a defensive position— "this has to to with me" or "this does not have to do with me"—is produced.[8] But the students, as we have seen, are more fluid in their multiple affiliations. There is a type of desire that gives them a theory of fluidity that may or may not be misguided. It may also suggest the need for a more sophisticated language so that these youth can begin to name their experiences and what it is that they want. Perhaps one of the biggest ironies in all of this, however, is that it is only through debating one's relation to something that one can get to know oneself. Throughout this ethnography cultural identity is not simply a network of constraining traditions, beliefs, and practices through which ethnic and other subjects are produced. It is a more complex process of negotiating, often in ambivalent ways, the discourses through which discursive subjects are made. Identity claims are made in multiple directions. They are also split between who one is and who one is not.

Let me now return to the three concepts, globalization, diaspora and difference, and the relationships between them. As indicated in chapter 1, the dynamics subsumed by globalization have changed the arena in which questions of culture, race, and identity are posed. Globalization reaches much further back in time than the end of the twentieth century, and the changing waves of immigration that affect the area of Maple Heights and make the global city of Toronto are linked to this history of globalization. Globalization paradoxically commodifies different cultures as temporally and spatially distinct while at the same time invoking notions of cultural hybridity and flux. The desire to know the many cultures of "the fifty-seven varieties" (as one teacher put it) who occupy the new multicultural context of Maple Heights is premised on theories of culture as temporally and spatially bounded. But at Maple Heights the youth are also invested in the other side of globalization, the cultural flows and the elusive cultures of youth that circulate globally that are not readily contained by the paradigm of folk culture. Again here we might observe a knowledge gap in the two ways of knowing and experiencing culture.

Diasporic identities also change under these circumstances when globalization becomes a question of home and belonging. As we have seen, students at Maple Heights have multiple place associations that are invoked in their talk of identity. Recall, for example, the student who sees himself as a deejay in Toronto in relation to how he imagines the deejay scene "back home" in Jamaica, or the student who comes to understand herself in Toronto in relation to the events unfolding in her former or "other" home of the Dominican Republic and its neighboring state of Haiti. These imagined homes and multiple place associations help shape identity and culture as experiences, and those experiences also transcend understandings of culture and identity as fixed or as locked into place. Following others I have drawn upon the concept *routes* rather than *roots* as a way of thinking about the differences between culture as fixed attributes and culture as a process—between fixity and flows.[9] The *routes* and *roots* metaphor must not, however, be understood as a binary because these concepts are mutually intertwined. The play of these concepts—uprooting, being en route, rerouting, intertwining roots—helps us to engage the complex ways of belonging and becoming. The concepts also help us reflect upon notions of diasporic identities in relation to questions of national identity and territorial attachments. Recall here the teacher who is concerned about what Canada is becoming because, she claims, "it has to be more than a collection of differences." At stake in this claim is how the community of nation is imagined, to recall Benedict Anderson, and what is being summoned in the process of imagining.[10] The youth in this study are also invested in a sense of belonging and of making a place for themselves within and as an integral part of the nation, but for them globalization opens up other ways of belonging. Their sense of nationhood is not necessarily a discrete and bounded entity, nor a fixed and unitary sense of identity to which the sentiments of their teachers seem to aspire. Instead globalization, diaspora, and difference act in such ways that these subjects can be seen to transcend the idea of an absolutist national identity and culture in favor of a set of experiences that connect them. In this way they forge communities and a sense of belonging through differences rather than conformity. Like youth elsewhere, this sense of belonging allows, as Alexander puts it, "a fluid and negotiable definition of identity which is tied primarily to the assumption of shared experience rather than place."[11] This means that the youth can belong and be Canadian in many different ways.

Throughout the research and writing of this book I have worked with but also against dominant discourses that set up the binaries of culture and subculture, dominant culture and minority culture, nation and ethnics. This has meant working with attribute theory of culture while at the same time offering a critique of the attributes suggested by such categories by placing them in tension with the inconsistencies, contradictions, and ambivalence through which those attributes are lived. In so doing I draw attention to how difference works in two ways. First, it functions in sociological thinking and planning to designate the shared experiences and networks of meanings as discrete and different groups and cultures. The student who observes "all the different cultures" in the school hallway, as well as the teachers who want to know these cultures, invoke this notion of difference. This understanding of difference, I have argued, relies on an understanding of culture as the social attributes that distinguish groups. It has come to frame ethnographic studies of subcultures, ethnic cultures, and so on. In this framework, difference is about similitude. However, throughout this study of elusive culture and questions of race and identity another kind of difference constantly intervenes to unsettle the assumptions about similitude upon which this first notion of difference is premised. While we see students being given as well as laying claim to all the different identity and cultural categories, the categories offer no guarantee for what their desires, social practices, and relations are or what they are becoming. Far from being predictable, throughout this study desires, social relations, and everyday cultural practices emerge as complex—full of surprises, tensions, contradictions, and ambivalence. And so to return to my question of why study students' experiences of race, gender, and culture, it is because such a study opens up opportunities for engaging the complexities and incompleteness of everyday social life without trying to domesticate its incongruities for the sake of theoretical coherence. After all, it is the incoherence, the elusiveness, and the spaces of ambivalence and contradictory claims that attract our theories in the first place.

Notes

Chapter 1: Mapping The Field

1. This name and all others used in this book, including names given to individuals in subsequent chapters, are fictive. Any resemblance to actual places and names is coincidental.

2. Paul Gilroy, "Cultural Studies and Ethnic Absolutism," in *Cultural Studies*, ed. Lawrence Grossberg, Cary Nelson, and Paula Treichler (New York: Routledge, 1992), 187–98.

3. Kobena Mercer, "'1968': Periodizing Postmodern Politics and Identity," in *Cultural Studies*, 424. Mercer observes that identity is an issue only when it is in crisis.

4. Anthony Giddens, *Profiles and Critiques in Social Theory* (Berkeley: University of California Press, 1982).

5. Diane Macdonell, *Theories of Discourse: An Introduction* (Oxford: Basil Blackwell, 1991); Deborah Tannen, *Conversational Style: Analyzing Talk Among Friends* (Norwood, N.J.: Ablex, 1984); Deborah Tannen, ed., *Framing in Discourse* (New York: Oxford University Press, 1993); Michael Silverstein and Greg Urban, eds., *Natural Histories of Discourse* (Chicago: University of Chicago Press, 1996); Renato Rosaldo, *Culture and Truth: The Remaking of Social*

137

Analysis (Boston: Beacon Press, 1989); Jacques Derrida, *Of Grammatology*, trans. Gayatri Chakravorty Spivak (Baltimore: The Johns Hopkins University Press, 1976).

6. Michel Foucault, *Power/Knowledge: Selected Interviews and Other Writings, 1972–1977*, ed. and trans. Colin Gordon (New York: Pantheon Books, 1981); Luther H. Martin, Huck Gutman, and H. Hutton, eds., *Technologies of the Self: A Seminar with Michel Foucault* (Amherst: University of Massachusetts Press, 1988).

7. Barry Smart, *Foucault: Marxism and Critique* (London: Routledge and Kegan Paul, 1983), 81–87.

8. Pierre Bourdieu, *The State Nobility: Elite Schools in the Field of Power* (Palo Alto: Stanford University Press, 1996); Samuel Bowles and Herbert Gintis, *Schooling in Capitalist America: Educational Performance and the Contradictions of Economic Life* (New York: Basic Books, 1976).

9. Mikhail Bakhtin, *The Dialogic Imagination: Four Essays*, ed. Michael Holquists, trans. Caryl Emerson and Michael Holquist (Austin: University of Texas Press, 1990); Deborah P. Britzman, *Practice Makes Practice: A Critical Study of Learning to Teach* (Albany: State University of New York Press, 1991).

10. Clifford Geertz, *The Interpretation of Cultures: Selected Essays* (New York: Basic Books, 1973), 5.

11. Bob Teasdale and Jennie Teasdale, eds., *Voices in a Seashell: Education, Culture and Identity* (Suva, Fiji: Institute of Pacific Studies, University of the South Pacific in association with UNESCO, 1992), 2.

12. Michele Fine, "Working the Hyphens—Reinventing the Self and Other in Qualitative Research," in *Handbook of Qualitative Research*, ed. Norman K. Denzin and Yvonna S. Lincoln (London: Sage Publications, 1994), 70–82.

13. James Clifford, "Introduction: Partial Truths," in *Writing Culture: The Poetics and Politics of Ethnography*, ed. James Clifford and George E. Marcus (Berkeley: University of California Press, 1986), 1–26.

14. Raymond Williams, *Culture* (London: Fontana Paperbacks, 1981), 10.

15. Roy Wagner, *The Invention of Culture* (Chicago: University of Chicago Press, 1981), 133ff.

16. Edward B. Tylor, *Primitive Culture: Researches into the Development of Mythology, Philosophy, Religion, Language, Art, and Custom* (London: Murray, 1891), 1.

17. Bronislaw Malinowski, *A Scientific Theory of Culture and Other Essays* (Chapel Hill: University of North Carolina Press, 1944), 38; Ruth Benedict, *Patterns of Culture* (Boston: Houghton Mifflin, 1959); Edward Sapir, "Culture, Genuine and Spurious," in *Selected Writings of Edward Sapir in Language and Personality* (Berkeley: University of California Press, 1985 [1924]), 308–31.

18. Edward Said, "Anthropology's Interlocutors: Re-presenting the Colonized," *Critical Inquiry* 15 (1989): 205–25; Said, *Orientalism* (New York: Vintage Books, 1979). Also see Carol Breckenridge and Peter van der Veer, eds., *Orientalism and the Postcolonial Predicament: Perspectives on South Asia* (Philadelphia: University of Pennsylvania Press, 1993); Nicholas Thomas, "Anthropology and Orientalism," *Anthropology Today* 7, no. 2 (1991): 4–7; Elazar Berken, "Rethinking Orientalism: Representations of 'Primitives' in Western Culture at the Turn of the Century," *History of European Ideas* 15, nos. 4–6 (1992): 759–65; B. S. Turner, *Orientalism, Postmodernism and Globalization* (London: Routledge, 1994); Benedict Anderson, *Imagined Communities: Reflections on the Origins and Spread of Nationalism* (London: Verso, 1993); Johanes Fabian, *Time and the Other: How Anthropology Makes its Object* (New York: Columbia University Press, 1983).

19. Clifford Geertz, *Works and Lives: The Anthropologist as Author* (Palo Alto, Calif.: Stanford University Press, 1988).

20. Wagner, *The Invention of Culture*, 16.

21. Toni Morrison, *Playing in the Dark: Whiteness and the Literary Imagination* (Cambridge: Harvard University Press, 1992), 17.

22. Geertz, *The Interpretation of Cultures*.

23. For example, Marvin Harris, *Beyond the Myths of Culture: Essays in Cultural Materialism* (London: Academic Press, 1980); Harris, *Cultural Materialism: The Struggle for a Science of Culture*

(New York: Random House, 1979); Harris, *Cannibals and Kings: The Origins of Culture* (New York: Random House, 1977); William Roseberry, *Anthropologies and Histories: Essays in Culture, History, and Political Economy* (New Brunswick, N.J.: Rutgers University Press, 1989); Eric Wolf, *Europe and the People Without History* (Berkeley: University of California Press, 1982); Paul Willis, *Learning to Labour: How Working-Class Kids Get Working-Class Jobs* (New York: Columbia University Press, 1981); Douglas E. Foley, *Learning Capitalist Culture: Deep in the Heart of Tejas* (Philadelphia: University of Pennsylvania Press, 1990).

24. George E. Marcus and Michael M. J. Fisher, eds., *Anthropology as Cultural Critique: An Experimental Moment in the Human Sciences* (Chicago: University of Chicago Press, 1986); Clifford and Marcus, eds.,*Writing Culture*); James Clifford, *The Predicament of Culture* (Cambridge: Harvard University Press, 1988); Mike Featherstone, *Undoing Culture: Globalization, Postmodernism and Identity* (London: Sage, 1995); Featherstone, *Consumer Culture and Postmodernism* (London: Sage, 1991); Featherstone, ed., *Postmodernism* (London: Sage, 1988); Jefferey Alexander and Steven Seidman, eds., *Culture and Society: Contemporary Debates* (Cambridge: Cambridge University Press, 1990); Ben Agger, *Culture Studies vs. Cultural Theory* (London: Falmer Press, 1992); George E. Marcus and Fred R. Myers, eds., *The Traffic in Culture: Refiguring Art and Anthropology* (Berkeley: University of California Press, 1995); Penelope Harvey, *Hybrids of Modernity: Anthropology, the Nation State and the Universal Exhibition* (London: Routledge, 1996); Barry Smart, *Postmodernity: Key Ideas* (London: Routledge, 1993); Stuart Hall, David Held, and Tony McGrew, eds., *Modernity and Its Futures* (Cambridge: Polity Press in association with the Open University, 1992); Scott Lash and Jonathan Friedman, eds., *Modernity and Identity* (Oxford: Blackwell, 1992); David Morley and Kevin Robins, *Spaces of Identity: Global Media, Electronic Landscapes and Cultural Boundaries* (London: Routledge, 1995); James Duncan and David Ley, eds., *Place/Culture/Representation*(London: Routledge, 1993).

25. Deborah P. Britzman, "Is There a Queer Pedagogy? Or Stop Reading Straight," *Educational Theory* 45, no. 2 (1995): 151; Britzman, "'The Question of Belief': Writing Poststructural Ethnography," *International Journal of Qualitative Studies in*

Education 8, no. 3 (1995): 229; Richard G. Fox, ed., *Recapturing Anthropology: Working in the Present* (Santa Fe, N. Mex.: School of American Research Press, 1991); George E. Marcus, "What Comes (Just) After 'Post'? The Case of Ethnography," in *Handbook of Qualitative Research*, ed. Norman K. Denzin and Yvonna S. Lincoln, 563–74; Paul Rabinow, *Reflections on Fieldwork in Morocco* (Berkeley: University of California Press, 1977).

26. Joan Ferrante et al., eds., *The Social Construction of Race and Ethnicity in the United States* (New York: Longman, 1988); Ruth Frankenberg, *White Women, Race Matters: The Social Construction of Whiteness* (Minneapolis: University of Minnesota Press, 1993); Peter M. E. Figueroa, *Education and the Social Construction of "Race"* (London: Routledge, 1991).

27. Edward Said, "Narrative and Geography," *New Left Review* 180 (1990): 81–100; Said, "Anthropology's Interlocutors"; Said, "Orientalism Reconsidered," in *Literature, Politics and Theory: Papers from the Essex Conference, 1976–84*, ed. Francis Barker et al. (London: Methuen, 1986), 210–19; Said, *Orientalism* (New York: Vintage Books, 1979); Breckenridge and van der Veer, eds., *Orientalism and the Postcolonial Predicament*; Nicholas Thomas, "Anthropology and Orientalism"; Berken, "Rethinking Orientalism"; Gen Doy, "Out of Africa: Orientalism, 'Race,' and the Female Body," *Body and Society* 2, no. 4 (1996): 17–44; B. S. Turner, *Orientalism, Postmodernism, and Globalization*; Wang Ning, "Orientalism versus Occidentalism?", *New Literary History* 28, no. 1 (1997): 57–67.

28. David Theo Goldberg, *Racial Subjects: Writing on Race in America* (New York: Routledge, 1997); Goldberg, *Racist Culture: Philosophy and the Politics of Meaning* (Oxford, U.K., and Cambridge, U.S: Blackwell, 1993); Goldberg, "The Semantics of Race," *Ethnic and Racial Studies* 15, no. 4 (1992): 543–69; Catherine Gimelli Martin, "Orientalism and the Ethnographer: Said, Herodotus, and the Discourse of Alterity," *Criticism* 32, no. 4 (1990): 511–30; Steven Gregory and Roger Sanjek eds., *Race* (New Brunswick, N.J.: Rutgers University Press, 1994).

29. Michael P. Banton, *Racial Theories*, 2d ed. (Cambridge: Cambridge University Press, 1998); Banton, *The Race Concept* (Newton Abbot, U.K.: David and Charles, 1975).

30. Eric Wolf, "Perilous Ideas: Race, Culture, People," *Current Anthropology* 35, no. 1 (1994): 1–11; Marie M. de Lepervanche, *Indians in a White Australia: An Account of Race, Class, and Indian Immigration to Eastern Australia* (Sydney: Allen & Unwin, 1984); Gill Bottomley and Marie de Lepervanche, eds., *Ethnicity, Class and Gender in Australia* (Sydney: Allen & Unwin, 1988).

31. Barbara Amiel, "Racism: An Excuse for Riots and Theft, *Macleans Magazine*, 19 May 1992, 15; Martin Barker, *The New Racism: Conservatives and the Ideology of the Tribe* (London: Junction Books, 1981); Frank Reeves, *British Racial Discourse* (Cambridge: Cambridge University Press, 1983); Jeffrey Case, *The New Racism in Europe: A Sicilian Ethnography* (New York: Cambridge University Press, 1987).

32. Hall, "The Question of Cultural Identity," in *Modernity and its Futures*, ed. Hall, Held, and McGrew, 276.

33. Erving Goffman, *Stigma: Notes on the Management of Spoiled Identity* (Englewood Cliffs, N.J.: Prentice-Hall, 1963); George Herbert Mead, *Mind, Self and Society* (Chicago: University of Chicago Press, 1934).

34. Hall, "The Question of Cultural Identity," 277.

35. Hall, "Cultural Identity and Diaspora," in *Identity: Community, Culture, Difference*, ed. Jonathan Rutherford (London: Lawrence and Wishart, 1990), 222–37. Debates on postmodernism are of relevance to these ways of talking about identity. Zygmunt Bauman (*Modernity and Ambivalence* [Cambridge: Polity Press, 1991], 272) describes postmodernism as modernity coming of age and looking at itself from a distance and discarding what it was once unconsciously doing. However, postmodernism is not a coherent body of theory but rather a wide-ranging and often conflicting set of claims and positions on the state of the world at the closing decade of the twentieth century. F. Jameson (*Postmodernism or the Cultural Logic of Late Capitalism* [London: Verso, 1991]), for example, argues that postmodernism should be seen as the logic of late capitalism while Baudrillard (*Jean Baudrillard: Selected Writings*, ed. M. Poster [Stanford, Calif.: Stanford University Press, 1988]) suggests that it signals a radical break with the past. Some (E. Laclau and C. Mouffe, *Hegemony*

and Socialist Strategy: Towards a Radical Democratic Politics [London: Verso, 1985]) argue that postmodernity offers possibilities for radical politics, while others suggest that it detracts from possibilities of political action and change (Alex Callinicos, *Against Postmodernism: A Marxist Critique* [New York: St. Martin's Press, 1990]; Gordon Lewis, *Main Currents in Caribbean Thought: The Historical Evolution of the Caribbean in Ideological Aspects, 1492–1900* [Baltimore: Johns Hopkins University Press, 1993]). For the purpose of this study of race and identity among high school youth, I take from postmodernism the impossibility of closures and the possibilities for working with the multiple intersections and contradictions of identity that modernity might construct as pathological, but that postmodernism views as normal. In place of grand or metatheories, postmodernist thought insists on a plurality of discourses and pays attention to "other world" and "other voices" such as those of women, gays, youth, and colonial and postcolonial subjects (see Kenneth Thompson, "Social Pluralism and Post-Modernity," in *Modernity and its Futures*, ed. Hall, Held, and McGrew, 227). Postmodernism does not just tolerate but is also engaged with ambivalence, ambiguity, and partiality in the making of identities. It also calls attention to how talk and writing bring order to what is lived as quite disorderly, unstable and complex (see Jane Flax, "Post-modernism and Gender Relations in Feminist Theory," *Signs* 12, no. 4 (1987): 621–43; Steven Seidman, *Difference Troubles: Queering Social Theory and Sexual Politics* [Cambridge: Cambridge University Press, 1997]).

36. Stuart Hall, "The West and the Rest: Discourse and Power," in *Formations of Modernity*, ed. Stuart Hall and Bram Gieben (Cambridge: Open University Press, 1992), 232–75.

37. Ulrich Beck, Anthony Giddens, and Scott Lash, *Reflexive Modernization: Politics, Tradition and Aesthetics in the Modern Social Order* (Cambridge: Polity Press, 1994); Anthony Giddens, *The Consequences of Modernity* (Cambridge: Polity Press, 1991); Penelope Harvey, *Hybrids of Modernity*; David Harvey, *The Condition of Postmodernity: An Enquiry into the Origins of Cultural Change* (Oxford: Basil Blackwell, 1989); Donna Haraway, "The Promises of Monsters: A Regenerative Politics for Inappropriate/d Others,"

in *Cultural Studies*, ed. Grossberg et al. (New York: Routledge, 1992), 295–337; Doreen B. Massey and P. M. Jess, *A Place in the World?: Places, Cultures and Globalization* (Oxford: Oxford University Press in association with the Open University, 1995); Massey, "A Place Called Home," *New Formations* 17 (1992): 3–15; Massey, "A global Sense of Place," *Marxism Today*, June 1991, 25–26; Massey, *Spatial Divisions of Labour: Social Structures and the Geography of Production* (London: Macmillan, 1984); Angelika Bammer, ed., *Displacements: Cultural Identities in Question* (Bloomington: Indiana University Press, 1994) ; Linda Basch, Nina Glick Schiller, and Christina Szanton Blanc, *Nations Unbound: Transnational Projects, Postcolonial Predicaments, and Deterritorialized Nation-States* (Langhorne, Pa.: Gordon and Breach, 1994); Massey, *Space, Place and Gender* (Cambridge: Polity Press, 1994); Akhil Gupta and James Ferguson, eds., *Culture, Power, Place: Explorations in Critical Anthropology* (Durham, N.C.: Duke University Press, 1997).

38. Arjun Appadurai, *Modernity at Large: Cultural Dimensions of Globalization* (Minneapolis: University of Minnesota Press, 1997); Ulf Hannerz, "Notes on the Global Ecumene," *Public Culture* 1, no. 2 (1989): 66–75; R. Thornton, "The Rhetoric of Ethnographic Holism," *Cultural Anthropology* 3, no. 3 (1988): 285–303; Marcus and Fisher, *Anthropology as Cultural Critique*.

39. Hall, "The Question of Cultural Identity," 300.

40. Massey, *Space, Place and Gender*, 115.

41. Avtar Brah, *Cartographies of Disapora: Contesting Identities* (London: Routledge, 1997), 209.

42. Tony Morrison, *Playing in the Dark*.

43. Jonathon Rutherford, ed., *Identity: Community, Culture, Difference* (London: Lawrence and Wishart, 1990), 10.

44. Diana Fuss, *Identification Papers* (New York: Routledge, 1995).

45. Jonathan Rutherford, "A Place Called Home: Identity and the Cultural Politics of Difference," in *Identity: Community, Culture, Difference*, ed. Rutherford, 10.

46. Kogila Moodley, *State Responses to Immigration in Culturally*

Homogeneous and Multicultural Societies: Comparative Perspectives (Toronto: University of Toronto Press, 1996).

47. Ronald Samuda, "The Canadian Brand of Multiculturalism: Goals and Educational Implications," in *Multicultural Education: The Interminable Debate*, ed. Sohan Modgil et al. (London: Falmer Press, 1986), 106.

48. Jean Burnet, "Myths and Multiculturalism," in *Multiculturalism in Canada: Social and Educational Perspectives*, ed. Samuda, Berry, and Laferriere (Toronto: Allyn and Bacon, 1975); See John A. Porter, *The Vertical Mosaic: An Analysis of Social Class and Power in Canada* (Toronto: University of Toronto Press, 1965), for an analysis of the imbalances of power and equality that marked the 'cultural mosaic'.

49. The field of research on this subject is large. But see, for example, John R. Mallea and Jonathan C. Young, *Cultural Diversity and Canadian Education: Issues and Innovations* (Ottawa: Carleton University Press, 1984); Barb Thomas, "Anti-racist Education: A response to Manicom," in *Breaking the Mosaic*, ed. Jon Young (Toronto: Garamond Press, 1987), 104–107; G. Brant, *The Realization of Anti-Racist Education* (London: Falmer Press, 1986); James A. Banks and Cherry A. McGee Banks, eds., *Multicultural Education : Issues and Perspectives*, 2d ed. (Boston: Allyn and Bacon, 1993); Chris Mullard, "The State's Response to Racism: Towards a Relational Explanation," in *Community Work and Racism*, ed. A. Ohri, B. Manning, and P. Curno (London: Routledge, 1982), 45–60; David Gillborn, *Racism and Antiracism in Real Schools: Theory, Policy, Practice* (Buckingham, U.K.: Open University Press, 1995).

50. David Gillborn, *"Race," Ethnicity, and Education: Teaching and Learning in Multi-ethnic Schools* (London: Unwin Hyman, 1990); Robert Jeffcoate, *Ethnic Minorities and Education* (London: Harper & Row, 1984); James Donald and Ali Rattansi, eds., *"Race," Culture and Difference*, (London: Sage Publications in association with the Open University, 1992); Peter Braham, Ali Rattansi and Richard Skellington, eds., *Racism and Antiracism: Inequalities, Opportunities, and Policies* (London: Sage Publications in association with The Open University, 1992): Paul Gilroy, *There Ain't No Black in the Union Jack* (Chicago: University of Chicago Press, 1991).

51. Paul Gilroy, *The Black Atlantic: Modernity and Double Consciousness* (Cambridge: Harvard University Press, 1993), 56.

52. Jonathan Friedman, *Cultural Identity and Global Process* (London: Sage Publications, 1994), 73.

53. Philip Cohen, "'It's Racism What Dunnit: Hidden Narratives in Theories of Racism," in *"Race," Culture and Difference,* ed. James and Rattansi (London: Sage, 1992), 63. See also Gyatri Spivak's notion of "strategic essentialism" (*The Post-Colonial Critic: Interviews, Strategies, Dialogues,* ed. Sarah Harasym [London: Routledge, 1990]) as well as Rattansi and Boyne's insistence on social formations around such categories as *Black* or *feminist* in order to achieve specific goals (Roy Boyne and Ali Rattansi, eds., *Postmodernism and Society* [Basingstoke, U.K.: Macmillan Education, 1990]); Rinaldo Walcott, *Black Like Who? Writing Black Canada* (Toronto: Insomniac Press, 1997) offers interesting discussion of what these categories might comprise.

54. Renato Rosaldo, "From the Door of His Tent: The Fieldworker and the Inquisitor," in *Writing Culture,* ed. Clifford and Marcus (Berkeley: University of California Press, 1986).

55. Said, *Culture and Imperialism* (London: Chatto and Windus, 1993); Said, "Europe and Its Others: An Arab Perspective," in *Visions of Europe,* ed. R. Kearney (Dublin: Wolfhound Press, 1992), 107–16; Said, "Anthropology's Interlocutors"; Said, "Identity, Negation, and Violence," *New Left Review* 171 (1988): 46–60; Said, "Reflections on Exile," *Granta* 13 (1984): 157–72; Said, *Covering Islam: How the Media and the Experts Determine How We See the Rest of the World* (New York: Pantheon Books, 1981); Said, *Orientalism*; Spivak, *The Post-Colonial Critic*; Spivak, *Marxism and the Interpretation of Culture* (Urbana: University of Illinois Press, 1988), 271–313; Spivak, *In Other Worlds: Essays in Cultural Politics* (NewYork: Methuen, 1987); Robert J. C. Young, *Colonial Desire: Hybridity in Theory, Culture and Race* (New York: Routledge, 1995); Young, *White Mythologies: Writing, History, and the West* (London: Routledge, 1990); N. B. Dirks, *The Hollow Crown: Ethnohistory of an Indian Kingdom* (Cambridge: Cambridge University Press, 1987); Dirks, ed., *Colonialism and Culture* (Ann Arbor: University of Michigan Press, 1992); N. B. Dirks, Geoff Eley and Sherry B. Ortner, eds.,

Culture/Power/History: A Reader in Contemporary Social Theory (Princeton: Princeton University Press, 1994); Ashis Nandy, *The Savage Freud and Other Essays on Possible and Retrievable Selves* (Princeton: Princeton University Press, 1995); Nandy, *The Illegitimacy of Nationalism: Rabindranath Tagore and the Politics of Self* (Delhi: Oxford University Press, 1994); Nandy, "The Political Culture of the Indian State," *Daedalus* 118, no. 4 (1989):1–26; Nandy, *The Tao of Cricket: On Games of Destiny and the Destiny of Games* (New York: Viking, 1989); Nandy, *The Intimate Enemy: Loss and Recovery of Self under Colonialism* (Delhi: Oxford University Press, 1988); Nandy, *Traditions, Tyranny and Utopias: Essays in the Politics of Awareness* (Delhi: Oxford University Press, 1987); Nandy, *Alternative Sciences: Creativity and Authenticity in Two Indian Scientists* (New Delhi: Allied, 1980); Nandy, *At the Edge of Psychology: Essays in Politics and Culture* (Delhi: Oxford University Press, 1980); Merryl Wyn Davies, Ashis Nandy, and Ziauddin Sardar, *Barbaric Others: A Manifesto of Western Racism* (London: Pluto Press, 1993); Raymond Lee Owens and Ashis Nandy, *The New Vaisyas* (Bombay: Allied, 1977); Nandy, ed., *Science, Hegemony and Violence: A Requiem for Modernity* (Tokyo: United Nations University; Delhi: Oxford University Press, 1988).

56. Appadurai, "Theory in Anthropology: Center and Periphery," *Comparative Studies in Society and History* 28, no. 2 (1986): 356–61; Hannerz, "Notes on the Global Ecumene"; Gilles Deleuze and Félix Guattari, *A Thousand Plateaus: Capitalism and Schizophrenia*, trans. Brian Massumi (London: Athlone Press, 1987).

57. John Van Maanen, ed., *Representation in Ethnography* (London: Sage, 1995).

58. Britzman, "'The Question of Belief'"; While I recognize the limits of modernist ethnography, for this research I have been influenced by those theoretical orientations that have emerged in anthropology since the early 1970s. S. Ortner ("Theory in Anthropology Since the Sixties," *Comparative Studies in Society and History* 26, no. 1 [1986]:126–66) notes how the orientation of this time draws attention to praxis and an intimate relationship between theory and practice with a focus on doing, on agent, and on closer involvement of actors in the research project. In educa-

tion this is repeated in "action research," which rejects positivism's appeal to rationality and reason that often meant conformity to a priori sets of rules and systems of thought (see P. Lather, "Research as Praxis," *Harvard Educational Review* 56, no. 3 [1986]: 257–77; John Elliot, *Action Research for Education Change* [Milton Keynes, U.K.: Open University Press, 1991]; W. Carr and S. Kemmis, *Becoming Critical: Education, Knowledge and Action Research* [London: Falmer Press, 1986]). One of the aims of action research, however, is to eliminate the distortion and contradictions of social life, which my own emphasis on elusive culture recognizes is not possible. Nevertheless, I take from this field of research its emphasis on reflexivity and close involvement with the subjects of research.

59. Zero tolerance was the name given to a code of disciplinary procedures adopted by one of the boards of education in Toronto. It stated that violence would not be tolerated within the school system and that students would be expelled upon being found guilty of actions perceived as violent.

60. Paul Rabinow, "Representations are Social Facts: Modernity and Post-Modernity in Anthropology," in *Writing Culture*, ed. Clifford and Marcus, 234–61; Stephen A. Tyler, "Post-Modern Ethnography: From Document of the Occult to Occult Document," in *Writing Culture*, 126.

61. Marcus, "What Comes (Just) after 'Post'?" 563–74.

Chapter 2: The Discursive Space of Schooling

1. Quotations here are drawn from notes made on my first conversation with the school principal. As this chapter progresses I draw on other conversations with teachers. Consequently, all quotations from here onward are from teachers. I deliberately avoid using names in this chapter. This is because the main aim is to identify the discourses that are circulating and being reproduced rather than the individuals who are parties to this process.

2. Conversation with the school principal.

3. Homi K. Bhabha, *The Location of Culture* (London: Routledge, 1994), 82.

4. Crawford Young, ed., *Ethnic Diversity and Public Policy: A Comparative Inquiry* (New York: St. Martin's Press, 1998); Will Kymlicka, *Finding our Way: Rethinking Ethnocultural Relations in Canada* (Toronto: Oxford University Press, 1998); Cynthia Willett, ed., *Theorizing Multiculturalism: A Guide to the Current Debate* (Malden, Mass.: Blackwell, 1998); Yehudi O. Webster, *Against the Multicultural Agenda: A Critical Thinking Alternative* (Westport, Conn.: Praeger, 1997).

5. And fieldwork is placed in quotations because a school is not what was usually imagined when anthropologists talked about "going to the field."

6. Rabinow, "Representations are Social Facts"; Rosaldo, "From the Door of His Tent"; Tyler, "Post-Modern Ethnography."

7. George E. Marcus, "Past, Present and Emergent Identities: Requirements for Ethnographies of the Late Twentiety-Century Modernity," in *Modernity and Identity*, ed. Lash and Friedman.

8. The school's status changed from collegiate to high school, as I discuss below.

9. Bauman, *Modernity and Ambivalence*.

10. Thomas Walkom, "Winning Hearts of Quebecers Takes More Than Mass Love-Ins," *Toronto Star*, 28 October 1995, sec. C, 4.

11. Bhabha, *The Location of Culture*; Bhabha, "Frontlines/Borderpost," in *Displacements*, ed. Bammer, 269–72.

12. Goffman, *Stigma*.

13. Kelly Tonghill, "Root Out Racism, Schools Ordered," *Toronto Star*, 15 July 1993, sec. A, 1, 28; Jennifer Lewington, "Ontario Attacks Racism in Classroom," *Globe and Mail* (Toronto), 16 July 1993, sec. A, 6; Deborah McDougall, "Ontario Attacks Racism in Schools," *Winnipeg Free Press*, 17 July 1993, sec. A, 3.

Chapter 3: Portraits of Identity

1. Jacques Derrida, *Margins of Philosophy*, trans. Alan Bass (Chicago: University of Chicago Press, 1988), 7. See also Derrida, *Writing and Difference* (London: Routledge, 1981).

2. See Judith Butler, *Gender Trouble: Feminism and the Subversion of Identity* (New York: Routledge, 1990), 136–37. Butler describes how gender categories conceal discontinuities. The same structure applies to race and other identity categories.

3. Homi K. Bhabha, "Interrogating Identity," *ICA Documents 6, Identity: The Real Me* (London: ICA, 1987), 6.

4. Nestor Garcia Canclini, *Hybrid Cultures: Strategies for Entering and Leaving Modernity* (Minneapolis: University of Minnesota Press, 1995), 207.

5. Dick Hebdige, *Cut 'n mix: Culture, Identity, and Caribbean Music* (London and New York: Routledge, 1987).

6. I. Chambers, *Border Dialogues: Journeys in Postmodernism* (London and New York: Routledge, 1990), 79.

7. For a discussion of "roots" and "routes" see Chambers, *Border Dialogues*; David Chioni Moore, "Routes: Alex Haley's Roots and the Rhetoric of Genealogy" *Transition: An International Review* 64 (1994): 4–21; Norval Edwards, "Roots and Some Routes Not Taken: A Caribcentric Reading of the Black Atlantic," *Found Object* 4 (fall 1994): 27–35; Paul Gilroy, "Route Work: The Black Atlantic and the Politics of Exile," in *The Postcolonial Question*, ed. Ian Chambers and Lidia Curti (London and New York: Routledge, 1996), 17–29 .

8. Gilroy, "Cultural Studies and Ethnic Absolutism," 187–98.

9. Richard Dyer, *White* (New York: Routledge, 1997).

10. Fuss, *Identification Papers*.

Chapter 4: Talk of Race and Identity

1. This use of "landscapes" borrows from Appadurai's ("Global Ethnoscapes: Notes and Queries for Transnational Anthropology," ed. Fox, 191–210) concept *ethnoscape* in which "ethno" refers to the comingling of peoples from various places and backgrounds, while "scapes" captures the fluidity of those movements.

2. Bauman, *Modernity and Ambivalence*, 61.

3. Ibid.

4 Dyer, *White.*

5. W. E. B. Dubois, *The Souls of Black Folk* (New York: Fawcett Publications, 1961); Faye V. Harrison, "The Du Boisian Legacy in Anthropology," *Critique of Anthropology* 12, no. 3 (1992): 239–60.

6. See Frantz Fanon, *Black Skin, White Masks* (New York: Grove Press, 1967).

7. Daniel Yon, "Culture, Schooling, and Identity: What Will Be the Focus in the Focus Schools?" (paper presented on a panel entitled *The Educational Experiences of African Canadian Youth,* American Association for African Studies Annual Conference, Toronto, November 1994); Yon, "Schooling and the Politics of Identity: A Case Study of Caribbean Students in a Toronto High School," in *Forging Identities and Patterns of Development in Latin America and the Caribbean,* ed. H. Diaz, J. W. A. Rummens, and P. D. M. Taylor (Toronto: Canadian Scholars Press, 1990); Yon, "Identity and Difference in the Caribbean Diaspora: Case Study from Metropolitan Toronto," in *The Re-ordering of Culture; Latin America, the Caribbean, and Canada in the Hood,* ed. Alvina Ruprecht and Cecilia Taiana (Ottawa: Carleton University Press, 1995), 479–97.

8. Gilroy, *The Black Atlantic.*

9. Ibid., 87.

10. See Spivak (*The Post Colonial Critic*) for the concept *strategic essentialism* and her interview in which she discusses strategy over essentialism ("In a Word. Interview," in *The Essential Difference,* ed. Naomi Schor and Elizabeth Weed [Bloomington and Indianapolis: Indiana University Press, 1994]), 151–84.

11. E. Balibar and I. Wallerstein, *Race, Nation, Class: Ambiguous Identities,* trans. Chris Turner (London: Verso, 1991).

12. Gilroy, "Cultural Studies and Ethnic Absolutism," 187–98.

13. Stuart Hall, "The Local and the Global: Globalization and the World System," in *Culture, Globalization and the World System: Contemporary Conditions for the Representation of Identity,* ed. Anthony D. King (Binghamton: Department of Art History, State University of New York, 1991); Hall, "Old and New Identities, Old and New Ethnicities," in *Culture, Globalization and the World System,* ed. King; Fanon, *Black Skin, White Masks.*

14. Bhabha, "Interrogating Identity," 10, on the repetitious desire to recognize ourselves doubly.

15. Wolf, "Perilous Ideas: Race, Culture, People."

Chapter 5: Gendering Race and Racializing Gender

1. Lewis, *Main Currents in Caribbean Thought*.

2. Kobena Mercer, *Welcome to the Jungle: New Positions in Black Cultural Studies* (New York: Routledge, 1994); Mercer, "Welcome to the Jungle," in *Identity*, 43–71.

3. Dyer, *White*.

4. See Mercer, "Black Hair/Style Politics," *New Formations* 3 (winter 1987): 33–54.

5. Marlon Riggs, *Black is Black Ain't: A Personal Journey Through Black Identity*, Independent Television Service (San Francisco, CA: California Newsreel, 1995) videorecording.

Chapter 6: Toward an Understanding of Elusive Culture.

1. Geertz, *Interpretation of Culture*, 19.

2. Hall, "Cultural Identity and Diaspora."

3. I am anxious to avoid having this book confined by the label "postmodernist" because of the multiple interpretations that have been placed on this concept, as I indicate in footnote no. 35 to chapter 1, and because such a concept would oversimplify my project. Furthermore, there is an intrinsic connection between modernity and postmodernity. See Rattansi, "Western Racisms, Ethnicities, and Identities in a 'Postmodern' Frame," in *Racism, Modernity and Identity: On the Western Front*, ed. Rattansi and Sallie Westwood (Cambridge: Polity Press, 1994), 19. Nevertheless, my use of the word "evoke" here is influenced partly by Steven Tyler's account on postmodern ethnography, which he sees as "an evolved test consisting of fragments of discourse intended to evoke in the minds of readers and writer an

emergent fantasy of a possible world of commonsense reality." ("Post-Modern Ethnography," 125).

4. Anthony Giddens, *The Constitution of Society: Outline of the Theory of Structuration* (Berkeley: University of California Press, 1984); Michel de Certeau, *The Practice of Everyday Life*, trans. S. Rendall (Berkeley: University of California Press, 1984).

5. Bauman, *Modernity and Ambivalence*.

6. See for example Willis, *Learning to Labour*; Hebdige, *Cut 'n mix*; R. Patrick Solomon, *Black Resistance in High School: Forging a Separatist Culture* (Albany: State University of New York Press, 1992); Signithia Fordham, *Blacked Out: Dilemmas of Race, Identity, and Success at Capital High* (Chicago: University of Chicago Press, 1996).

7. Elaine Carey, "Is TO Tops in Diversity? It has at least 162 Ethnic Groups, Few Other Cities on Earth Come Close," *Toronto Star*, 11 June 1998, sec. G, 14, 16; Elaine Carey, "1 in 10 Canadians a Minority: Stats Can, and Almost Half Live in the Toronto Area," *Toronto Star*, 18 February 1998, sec. A, 1, 25; Lila Sarick, "Visible Minorities Flock to City: Special Needs of Students, Immigrant Communities Cited in Calls for More Provincial, Federal Dollars," *Globe and Mail* (Toronto), 18 February 1998; John Barber, "Different Colours, Changing City," *Globe and Mail* (Toronto), 20 February 1998, sec. A, 8.

8. I might note here that Jane, the student discussed in chapter four, did not attend a talk that I gave to her class during African History Month on the first war of resistance in Zimbabwe. She explained to me later that she decided not to attend because it had nothing to do with her. The same argument is reproduced by educators and others who make claims about certain literatures "belonging" to certain groups.

9. For example Gilroy, "Route Work"; Moore, "Routes"; Chambers, *Border Dialogues*; Hall "Cultural Identity and Diaspora"; and others cited in earlier chapters.

10. Anderson, *Imagined Communities*.

11. Alexander's work is a study of Black youth in Britain. See Claire Alexander, *The Art of Being Black* (Oxford: Clarendon Press, 1996).

Bibliography

Agger, Ben. *Culture Studies vs. Cultural Theory.* London: Falmer Press, 1992.

Alexander, Claire. *The Art of Being Black.* Oxford: Clarendon Press, 1996.

Alexander, Jefferey, and Steven Seidman, eds. *Culture and Society: Contemporary Debates.* Cambridge: Cambridge University Press, 1990

Amiel, Barbara. "Racism: An Excuse for Riots and Theft." *Macleans Magazine,* May 18, 1992, 15.

Anderson, Benedict. *Imagined Communities: Reflections on the Origin and Spread of Nationalism.* London: Verso, 1993.

Appadurai, Arjun. "Theory in Anthropology: Center and Periphery." *Comparative Studies in Society and History* 28, no. 2 (1986): 356–61.

———. "Global Ethnoscapes: Notes and Queries for Transnational Anthropology." In *Recapturing Anthropology: Working in the Present,* ed. Richard G. Fox, 191–210. Santa Fe, N. Mex.: School of American Research Press, 1991.

———. *Modernity at Large: Cultural Dimensions of Globalization.* Minneapolis: University of Minnesota Press, 1997.

Bakhtin, Mikhail. *The Dialogic Imagination: Four Essays.* Ed. Michael Holquist, trans. Caryl Emerson and Michael Holquist. Austin: University of Texas Press, 1990.

Balibar, E., and I. Wallerstein. *Race, Nation, Class: Ambiguous Identities.* Trans. Chris Turner. London:Verso, 1991.

Bammer, Angelika, ed. *Displacements: Cultural Identities in Question.* Bloomington: Indiana University Press, 1994.

Banks, James, and Cherry A. McGee Banks, eds. *Multicultural Education: Issues and Perspectives* 2d ed. Boston: Allyn and Bacon, 1993.

Banton, Michael P. *The Race Concept.* Newton Abbot, U.K.: David and Charles, 1975.

———. *Racial Theories,* 2d ed. Cambridge: Cambridge University Press, 1998.

Barber, John. "Different Colours, Changing City." *Globe and Mail* (Toronto), 20 February 1998, sec. A, 8.

Basch, Linda, Nina Glick Schiller, and Cristina Szanton Blanc. *Nations Unbound: Transnational Projects, PostColonial Predicaments and Deterritorialized Nation-States.* Langhorne, Pa.: Gordon and Breach, 1994.

Baudrillard, Jean. *Jean Baudrillard: Selected Writings.* Ed. M. Poster. Stanford, Ca.: Stanford University Press, 1988.

Bauman, Zygmunt. *Modernity and Ambivalence.* Cambridge: Polity Press, 1991.

Beck, Ulrich, Anthony Giddens, and Scott Lash. *Reflexive Modernization: Politics, Tradition, and Aesthetics in the Modern Social Order.* Cambridge: Polity Press, 1994.

Benedict, Ruth. *Patterns of Culture.* Boston: Houghton Mifflin and Co., 1959.

Berken, Elazar. "Rethinking Orientalism: Representations of 'Primitives' in Western Culture at the Turn of the Century." *History of European Ideas* 15, nos. 4–6: 759–65.

Bhabha, Homi. "Interrogating Identity." *ICA Documents 6. Identity: The Real Me,* 5–11, London: ICA, 1987.

———. "Frontlines/Borderpost." In *Displacements,* ed. Angelica Bammer, 269–72. Bloomington: Indiana University Press, 1994.

———. *The Location of Culture.* London: Routledge. 1994

Bottomley, Gill, and Marie. De Lepervanche, eds. *Ethnicity, Class and Gender in Australia.* Sydney: Allen & Unwin, 1988.

Bourdieu, Pierre. *The State Nobility: Elite Schools in the Field of Power.* Stanford: Stanford University Press, 1996.

Bowles, Samuel and Herbert Gintis. *Schooling in Capitalist America: Educational Reform and the Contradictions of Economic Life.* New York: Basic Books, 1976.

Boyne, R., and Ali Rattansi, eds. *Postmodernism and Society.* Basingstoke, U.K.: Macmillan Education, 1990.

Brah, Avtar. *Cartographies of Diaspora: Contesting Identities.* London: Routledge, 1997.

Braham, Peter, Ali Rattansi, and Richard Skellington, eds. *Racism and Antiracism: Inequalities, Opportunities, and Policies.* London: Sage Publications in association with the Open University, 1992.

Breckenridge, Carol, and Peter van der Veer, eds. *Orientalism and the Postcolonial Predicament: Perspectives on South Asia.* Philadelphia: University of Pennsylvania Press, 1993.

Britzman, Deborah. *Practice Makes Practice: A Critical Study of Learning to Teach.* Albany: State University of New York Press, 1991.

———. "'The Question of Belief': Writing Poststructural Ethnography." *International Journal of Qualitative Studies in Education* 8, no. 3 (1995): 229–38.

———. "Is There a Queer Pedagogy? Or Stop Reading Straight." *Educational Theory* 45, no. 2 (1995): 151.

Burnet, Jean. "Myths and Multiculturalism." In *Multiculturalism in Canada: Social and Educational Perspectives,* ed. Ronald J. Samuda, John W. Berry, and Michel Laferriere, 18–29. Toronto: Allyn and Bacon, 1964.

Butler, Judith. *Gender Trouble: Feminism and the Subversion of Identity.* New York: Routledge, 1990.

Callinicos, Alex. *Against Postmodernism: A Marxist Critique.* New York: St. Martin's Press, 1990.

Canclini, Nestor Garcia. *Hybrid Cultures: Strategies for Entering and Leaving Modernity.* Minneapolis: University of Minnesota Press, 1995.

Carey, Elaine. "1 in 10 Canadians a Minority: Stats Can, and About Half Live in the Toronto Area." *Toronto Star,* 18 February, 1998, sec. A, 1, 25.

———. "Is TO Tops in Diversity? It Has at Least 162 Ethnic Groups, Few Other Cities on Earth Come Close." *Toronto Star*, 11 June 1998, sec. G, 14, 16.

Carr, W., and S. Kemmis. *Becoming Critical: Education, Knowledge and Action Research*. London, Philadelphia: Falmer Press, 1986.

de Certeau, Michel. *The Practice of Everyday Life*. Trans. S. Rendall. Berkeley: University of California Press, 1984.

Chambers, I. *Border Dialogues: Journeys in Postmodernism*. London: Routledge, 1990.

Clifford, James. "Introduction: Partial Truths." In *Writing Culture: The Poetics and Politics of Ethnography*, ed. James Clifford and George E. Marcus, 1–26. Berkeley: University of California Press, 1986.

———. *The Predicament of Culture*. Cambridge, Mass.: Harvard University Press, 1988.

Cohen, Philip. "'It's Racism What Dunnit': Hidden Narratives in Theories of Racism." In *"Race," Culture, and Difference*, ed. James Donald and Ali Rattansi, 62–103. London: Sage Publications in association with the Open University, 1992.

Davies, Merryl Wyn, Ashis Nandy, and Ziauddin Sardar. *Barbaric Others: A Manifesto of Western Racism*. London: Pluto Press, 1993.

Deleuze, Gilles, and Felix Guattari. *A Thousand Plateaus: Capitalism and Schizophrenia*. Trans. Brian Massumi. London: Athlone Press, 1987.

Derrida, Jacques. *Of Grammatology*. Trans. Gayatri Chakravorty Spivak. Baltimore: The Johns Hopkins University Press, 1976.

———. *Writing and Difference*. Trans. Alan Bass. London: Routledge, 1981.

———. *Margins of Philosophy*. Trans. Alan Bass. Chicago: University of Chicago Press, 1998.

Dirks, N. B. *The Hollow Crown: Ethnohistory of an Indian Kingdom*. Cambridge: Cambridge University Press, 1987.

———. ed. *Colonialism and Culture*. Ann Arbor: University of Michigan Press, 1992.

Dirks, N. B., Geoff Eley, and Sherry B. Ortner, eds. *Culture/ Power/History: A Reader in Contemporary Social Theory*. Princeton: Princeton University Press, 1994.

Donald, James, and Ali Rattansi, eds. *"Race," Culture and Difference.* London: Sage Publications in association with the Open University, 1992.

Doy, Gen. "Out of Africa: Orientalism, 'Race' and the Female Body." *Body and Society* 2, no. 4 (1996): 17–44.

Dubois, W. E. B. *The Souls of Black Folk.* New York: Fawcett Publications, 1961.

Duncan, James, and David Ley, eds. *Place/Culture/Representation.* London: Routledge, 1993.

Dyer, Richard. *White.* New York: Routledge, 1997.

Edwards, Norval. "Roots and some Routes Not Taken: A Caribcentric Reading of the Black Atlantic." *Found Object* 4 (fall 1994): 27–35.

Elliot, John. *Action Research for Education Change.* Milton Keynes, U.K.: Open University Press, 1991.

Fabian, Johanes. *Time and the Other: How Anthropology Makes Its Object.* New York: Columbia University Press, 1983.

Fanon, Frantz. *Black Skin, White Masks.* New York: Grove Press, 1967.

Featherstone, M., ed. *Postmodernism.* London: Sage, 1988.

———. *Consumer Culture and Postmodernism.* London: Sage, 1991.

———. *Undoing Culture: Globalization, Postmodernism, and Identity.* London: Sage, 1995.

Ferrante, Joan, et al., eds. *The Social Construction of Race and Ethnicity in the United States.* New York: Longman, 1998.

Figueroa, Peter M. E. *Education and the Social Construction of "Race."'* London: Routledge, 1991.

Fine, Michele. "Working the Hyphens—Reinventing the Self and Other in Qualitative Research." In *Handbook of Qualitative Research*, ed. Norma K. Denzin and Yvonna S. Lincoln, 70–82. London: Sage Publications, 1994.

Flax, Jane. "Post-modernism and Gender Relations in Feminist Theory." *Signs* 12, no. 4, (1987).

Foley, Douglas E. *Learning Capitalist Culture: Deep in the Heart of Tejas.* Philadelphia: University of Pennsylvania Press, 1990.

Fordham, Signithia. *Blacked Out: Dilemmas of Race, Identity and Success at Capital High.* Chicago: University of Chicago Press, 1996.

Foucault, Michel. *Power/Knowledge: Selected Interviews and Other Writings, 1972–1977*. Ed. and trans. Colin Gordon. New York: Pantheon Books, 1981.

———. *Technologies of the Self: A Seminar with Michel Foucault*. Ed. Luther H. Martin, Huck Gutman, and H. Hutton. Amherst: University of Massachusetts Press, 1988.

Fox, Richard G., ed. *Recapturing Anthropology: Working in the Present*. Santa Fe, N. Mex.: School of American Research Press, 1991.

Frankenberg, Ruth. *White Women, Race Matters: The Social Construction of Whiteness*. Minneapolis: University of Minnesota Press, 1993.

Friedman, Jonathan. *Cultural Identity and Global Process*. London: Sage Publications, 1994.

Fuss, Diana. *Identification Papers*. New York: Routledge, 1995.

Geertz, Clifford. *The Interpretation of Cultures: Selected Essay*. New York: Basic Books, 1973.

———. *Works and Lives: The Anthropologist as Author*. Palo Alto, Calif.: Stanford University Press, 1973.

Giddens, Anthony. *Profiles and Critiques in Social Theory*. Berkeley and Los Angeles: University of California Press, 1982.

———. *The Constitution of Society: Outline of the Theory of Structuration*. Berkeley: University of California Press, 1984.

———. *The Consequences of Modernity*. Cambridge: Polity Press, 1991.

Gillborn, David. *"Race," Ethnicity and Education: Teaching and Learning in Multi-ethnic Schools*. London: Unwin Hyman, 1990.

———. *Racism and Antiracism in Real Schools: Theory, Policy, Practice*. Buckingham, U.K.: Open University Press, 1995.

Gilroy, Paul. "Cultural Studies and Ethnic Absolutism." In *Cultural Studies*, ed. Lawrence Grossberg, Cary Nelson and Paula Treichler, 187–98. New York, London: Routledge, 1992.

———. *The Black Atlantic: Modernity and Double Consciousness*. Cambridge: Harvard University Press, 1993.

Goffman, Erving. *Stigma: Notes on the Management of Spoiled Identity*. Englewood Cliffs, N.J.: Prentice-Hall, 1963.

Goldberg, David Theo. "The Semantics of Race." *Ethnic and Racial Studies* 15, no. 4 (1992): 543–69.

———. *Racist Culture: Philosophy and the Politics of Meaning.* Cambridge, Mass.: Blackwell, 1993.

———. *Racial Subjects: Writing on Race in America.* New York: Routledge, 1997.

Gupta, Akhil, and James Ferguson, eds. *Culture, Power, Place: Explorations in Critical Anthropology.* Durham, N.C.: Duke University Press, 1997.

Hall, Stuart. "Cultural Identity and Diaspora." In *Identity: Community, Culture, Difference,* ed. Jonathan Rutherford, 222–37. London: Lawrence & Wishart, 1990.

———. "The Local and the Global: Globalization and the World System." In *Culture, Globalization and the World System: Contemporary Conditions for the Representation of Identity,* ed. Anthony D. King. Binghamton: Dept. of Art and Art History, State University of New York at Binghamton, 1991.

———. "Old and New Identities, Old and New Ethnicities." In *Culture, Globalization and the World System,* ed. King.

———. "The Question of Cultural Identity." In *Modernity and Its Futures,* ed. Stuart Hall, David Held and Tony McGrew, 273–315. Cambridge: Polity Press in association with the Open University, 1992.

Hall, Stuart, David Held, and Tony McGrew, eds. *Modernity and its Futures.* Cambridge: Polity Press in association with the Open University, 1992.

Hannerz, Ulf. "Notes on the Global Ecumene." *Public Culture* 1, no. 2 (1989).

Haraway, Donna. "The Promises of Monsters: A Regenerative Politics for Inappropriate/d Others." In *Cultural Studies,* ed. Grossberg et al., 295–337. New York: Routledge, 1992.

Harris, Marvin. *The Rise of Anthropological Theory: A History of Theories of Culture.* New York: Harper & Row, 1968.

———. *Cannibals and Kings: The Origins of Culture.* New York: Random House, 1977.

———. *Cultural Materialism: The Struggle for a Science of Culture.* New York: Random House, 1979.

———. *Beyond the Myths of Culture: Essays in Cultural Materialism.* London: Academic Press, 1980.

162 — Bibliography

Harvey, David. *The Condition of Postmodernity: An Enquiry into the Origins of Cultural Change.* Oxford: Basil Blackwell, 1989.

Harvey, Penelope. *Hybrids of Modernity: Anthropology, the Nation State and the Universal Exhibition.* London: Routledge, 1996.

Hebdige, Dick. *Cut 'n' Mix: Culture, Identity, and Caribbean Music.* London, New York: Routledge, 1987.

Jameson, F. *Postmodernism or the Cultural Logic of Late Capitalism.* London: Verso, 1991.

Jeffcoate, Robert. *Ethnic Minorities and Education.* London: Harper & Row, 1984.

Kymlicka, Will. *Finding Our Way: Rethinking Ethnocultural Relations in Canada.* Toronto: Oxford University Press, 1998.

Laclau, E., and C. Mouffe. *Hegemony and Socialist Strategy: Towards a Radical Democratic Politics.* London: Verso, 1985.

Lash, Scott, and Jonathan Friedman, eds. *Modernity and Identity.* Oxford: Blackwell, 1992.

Lather, P. "Research as Praxis." *Harvard Educational Review* 56, no. 3 (1986): 257–77.

de Lepervanche, Marie. *Indians in a White Australia: An Account of Race, Class and Indian Immigration to Eastern Australia.* Sydney: Allen & Unwin, 1984.

Lewington, Jennifer. "Ontario Attacks Racism in Classroom," *Globe and Mail* (Toronto), 16 July 1993, sec. A, 6.

Lewis, Gordon. *Main Currents in Caribbean Thought: The Historical Evolution of the Caribbean in Its Ideological Aspects, 1492–1900.* Baltimore: Johns Hopkins University Press, 1993.

Macdonell, Diane. *Theories of Discourse: An Introduction.* Oxford: Basil Blackwell, 1991.

Malinowski, Bronislaw. *A Scientific Theory of Culture and Other Essays.* Chapel Hill: University of North Carolina Press, 1944.

Mallea, John R., and Jonathan C. Young. *Cultural Diversity and Canadian Education: Issues and Innovations.* Ottawa: Carleton University Press, 1984.

Marcus, George. "Past, Present and Emergent Identities: Requirements for Ethnographies of the Late Twentieth-Century Modernity." In *Modernity and Identity,* ed. Scott Lash and Jonathan Friedman. Oxford and Cambridge, Mass.: Blackwell, 1992.

———. 1994. "What Comes (Just) after 'Post'? The Case of Ethnography." In *Handbook of Qualitative Research,* ed. Norma K. Denzin and Yvonne S. Lincoln, 563–74. London: Sage Publications, 1994.

Marcus, George E., and Michael M. J. Fisher, eds. *Anthropology as Cultural Critique: An Experimental Moment in the Human Sciences.* Chicago: University of Chicago Press, 1986.

Marcus, George E. and Fred R. Myers, eds. *The Traffic in Culture: Refiguring Art and Anthropology.* Berkeley: University of California Press, 1995.

Martin, Catherine Gimelli. 1990. "Orientalism and the Ethnographer: Said, Herodotus, and the Discourse of Alterity." *Criticism* 32, no. 4 (1990): 511–30.

Massey, Doreen. *Spatial Divisions of Labour: Social Structures and the Geography of Production.* London: Macmillan, 1984.

———. "A Global Sense of Place." *Marxism Today* (June 1991): 25–26.

———. "A Place Called Home." *New Formations* 17 (1992): 3–15.

———. *Space, Place and Gender.* Cambridge: Polity Press, 1994.

Massey, Doreen, and P. M. Jess. *A Place in the World?: Places, Cultures and Globalization.* Oxford: Oxford University Press in association with the Open University, 1995.

McDougall, Deborah. "Ontario Attacks Racism in Schools," *Winnipeg Free Press,* 17 July 1993, sec. A, 3.

Mead, George Herbert. *Mind, Self and Society.* Chicago: University of Chicago Press, 1934.

Mercer, Kobena. "Black Hair/Style Politics," *New Formations* 3 (winter 1987): 33–54.

———. "Welcome to the Jungle." In *Identity: Community, Culture, Difference,* ed. Jonathan Rutherford, 43–71. London: Lawrence & Wishart, 1990.

———. "'1968': Periodizing Postmodern Politics and Identity." In *Cultural Studies,* ed. Grossberg et al. New York: Routledge, 1992.

———. *Welcome to the Jungle: New Positions in Black Cultural Studies.* New York and London: Routledge, 1994.

Moodley, Kogila. A. *State Responses to Immigration in Culturally Homogeneous and Multicultural Societies: Comparative Perspectives.* Toronto: University of Toronto Press, 1996.

Moore, David Chioni. 1994. "Routes: Alex Haley's Roots and the "Rhetoric of Genealogy." *Transition: An International Review* 64:4–21.

Morley, David, and Kevin Robins. *Spaces of Identity: Global Media, Electronic Landscapes and Cultural Boundaries.* London: Routledge, 1995.

Morrison, Toni. *Playing in the Dark: Whiteness and the Literary Imagination.* Cambridge: Harvard University Press, 1992.

Mullard, Chris. "The State's Response to Racism: Towards a Relational Explanation." In *Community Work and Racism*, ed. A. Ohri, B. Manning, and P. Curno, 45–59. London: Routledge, 1982.

Nandy, Ashis. *Alternative Sciences: Creativity and Authenticity in Two Indian Scientists.* New Delhi: Allied, 1980.

———. *At the Edge of Psychology: Essays in Politics and Culture.* Delhi: Oxford University Press, 1980.

———. *Traditions, Tyranny and Utopias: Essays in the Politics of Awareness.* Delhi: Oxford University Press, 1987.

———. *The Intimate Enemy: Loss and Recovery of Self Under Colonialism.* Delhi: Oxford University Press, 1988.

———. "The Political Culture of the Indian State." *Daedalus* 118, no. 4 (1989): 1–26.

———. *The Tao of Cricket: On Games of Destiny and the Destiny of Games.* New York: Viking, 1989.

———. *The Illegitimacy of Nationalism: Rabindranath Tagore and the Politics of Self.* Delhi: Oxford University Press, 1994.

———. *The Savage Freud and Other Essays on Possible and Retrievable Selves.* Princeton: Princeton University Press, 1995.

———, ed. *Science, Hegemony, and Violence: A Requiem for Modernity.* Tokyo: United Nations University; Delhi: Oxford University Press, 1988.

Ning, Wang. "Orientalism versus Occidentalism?" *New Literary History* 28, no. 1 (1997): 57–67.

Ortner, S. "Theory in Anthropology Since the Sixties." *Comparative Studies in Society and History* 26, no. 1 (1986): 121–66.

Owens, Raymond Leem and Ashis Nandy. *The New Vaisyas.* Bombay: Allied, 1977.

Porter, John A. *The Vertical Mosaic: An Analysis of Social Class and Power in Canada.* Toronto: University of Toronto Press, 1965.

Rabinow, Paul. *Reflections on Fieldwork in Morocco.* Berkeley: University of California Press, 1977.

———. "Representations are Social Facts: Modernity and Post-Modernity in Anthropology." In *Writing Culture: The Poetics and Politics of Ethnography,* ed. J. Clifford and G. Marcus, 234–61. Berkeley and London: University of California Press, 1986.

Rattansi, Ali. "Western Racisms, Ethnicities, and Identities in a 'Postmodern' Frame." In *Racism, Modernity and Identity: On the Western Front,* ed. Ali Rattansi and Sallie Westwood. Cambridge: Polity Press, 1994.

Riggs, Marlon. *Black is Black Ain't: A Personal Journey Through Black Identity,* Independent Television Service. San Francisco: California Newsreel. Videorecording.

Rosaldo, Renato. "From the Door of his Tent: The Fieldworker and the Inquisitor." In *Writing Culture: The Poetics and Politics of Ethnography,* ed. James Clifford and George E. Marcus. Berkeley and London: University of California Press, 1986.

———. *Culture and Truth: The Remaking of Social Analysis.* Boston: Beacon Press, 1989.

Roseberry, William. *Anthropologies and Histories: Essays in Culture, History, and Political Economy.* New Brunswick, N.J.: Rutgers University Press, 1989.

Rutherford, Jonathan, ed. *Identity: Community, Culture, Difference.* London: Lawrence & Wishart, 1990.

Said, Edward. *Orientalism.* New York: Vintage Books, 1979.

———. *Covering Islam: How the Media and the Experts Determine How We See the Rest of the World.* New York: Pantheon Books, 1981.

———. "Reflections on Exile." *Granta* 13 (1984): 157–72.

———. "Orientalism Reconsidered." In *Literature, Politics and Theory: Papers from the Essex Conference, 1976-84,* ed. Francis Barker et al., 210–29. London: Methuen, 1986.

———. "Identity, Negation and Violence." *New Left Review* 171 (1988): 46–60.

———. "Anthropology's Interlocutors: Representing the Colonized." *Critical Inquiry* 15 (1989): 205–25.

———. "Narrative and Geography." *New Left Review* 180 (1990): 81–100.

————. "Europe and Its Others: An Arab Perspective." In *Visions of Europe*, ed. R. Kearney, 107–16. Dublin: Wolfhound Press, 1992.

————. *Culture and Imperialism*. London: Chatto and Windus, 1993.

Samuda, R. 1986. "The Canadian Brand of Multiculturalism: Social Goals and Educational Implications." In *Multicultural Education: The Interminable Debate*, ed. S. Modgil et al., 101–10. London and Philadelphia: Falmer Press.

Sapir, Edward. "Culture, Genuine and Spurious." In *Selected Writings of Edward Sapir in Language and Personality*, 308–31. Berkeley: University of California Press, 1985.

Sarick, Lila. "Visible Minorities Flock to City: Special Needs of Students, Immigrant Communities Cited in Calls for More Provincial, Federal Dollars." *Globe and Mail* (Toronto), 18 February 1998, sec. A, 8.

Seidman, Steven. *Difference Troubles: Queering Social Theory and Sexual Politics*. Cambridge: Cambridge University Press, 1997.

Silverstein, Michael, and Greg Urban, eds. *Natural Histories of Discourse*. Chicago: University of Chicago Press, 1996.

Smart, Barry. *Foucault: Marxism and Critique*. London and Boston: Routledge and Kegan Paul, 1983.

————. *Postmodernity: Key Ideas*. London: Routledge, 1993.

Solomon, R. Patrick. *Black Resistance in High School: Forging a Separatist Culture*. Albany: State University of New York Press, 1992.

Spivak, Gyatri. *In Other Worlds: Essays in Cultural Politics*. New York: Methuen, 1987.

————. *Marxism and the Interpretation of Culture*. Urbana: University of Illinois Press, 1988.

————. *The Post-Colonial Critic: Interviews, Strategies, Dialogue*. Ed. Sarah Harasym. New York, London: Routledge, 1990.

Spivak, Gyatri, with Ellen Booney. "In a Word. Interview." In *The Essential Difference*, ed. Naomi Schor and Elizabeth Weed, 157–84. Bloomington and Indianapolis: Indiana University Press, 1994.

Tannen, Deborah. *Conversational Style: Analyzing Talk among Friends*. Norwood, N.J.: Ablex Publishing Company, 1984.

————, ed. *Framing in Discourse*. New York: Oxford University Press, 1993.

Teasdale, Bob, and Jennie Teasdale, eds. *Voices in a Seashell: Education, Culture and Identity*. Suva, Fiji: Institute of Pacific Studies, University of the South Pacific in association with UNESCO, 1992.

Thomas, Barb. "Anti-racist Education: A Response to Manicom." In *Breaking the Mosaic*, ed. Jon Young, 104–107. Toronto: Garamond Press, 1987.

Thomas, Nicholas. "Anthropology and Orientalism." *Anthropology Today* 7, no. 2 (1991).

Thompson, Kenneth. "Social Pluralism and Post-Modernity." In *Modernity and Its Futures*, ed. Stuart Hall, David Held and Tony McGrew, 221–72. Cambridge: Polity Press in Association with the Open University, 1992.

Thornton, R. "The Rhetoric of Ethnographic Holism." *Cultural Anthropology* 3, no. 3 (1988): 285–303.

Tonghill, Kelly. "Root Out Racism, Schools Ordered," *Toronto Star*, July 15, 1993, sec. A, 1, 28.

Turner, B. S. *Orientalism, Postmodernism and Globalization*. London: Routledge, 1994.

Tyler, Stephen A. "Post-Modern Ethnography: From Document of the Occult to Occult Document." In *Writing Culture: The Poetics and Politics of Ethnography*, ed. James Clifford and George E. Marcus, 122–40. Berkeley and London: University of California Press, 1986.

Tylor, Edward B. *Primitive Culture: Researches into the Development of Mythology, Philosophy, Religion, Language, Art, and Custom*. London: Murray, 1891.

Van Maanen, John, ed. *Representation in Ethnography*. London: Sage, 1995.

Wagner, Roy. *The Invention of Culture*. Chicago: University of Chicago Press, 1981.

Walkom, Thomas. "Winning Hearts of Quebecers Takes More Than Mass Love-Ins." *Toronto Star*, 28 October 1995, sec. C, 4.

Webster, Yehudi O. *Against the Multicultural Agenda: A Critical Thinking Alternative*. Westport, Conn.: Praeger, 1997.

Willett, Cynthia, ed. *Theorizing Multiculturalism: A Guide to the Current Debate*. Malden, Mass.: Blackwell, 1998.

Williams, Raymond. *Culture*. London: Fontana Paperbacks, 1981.

Willis, Paul. *Learning to Labour: How Working Class Kids Get Working Class Jobs*. New York: Columbia University Press, 1981.

Wolf, Eric. *Europe and the People Without History*. Berkeley: University of California Press, 1982.

———. "Perilous Ideas: Race, Culture, People." *Current Anthropology* 35, no. 1 (1994): 1–11.

Yon, D. "Schooling and the Politics of Identity: A Case Study of Caribbean Students in a Toronto High School." In *Forging Identities and Patterns of Development in Latin America and the Caribbean*, ed. H. Diaz, J. W. A. Rummens, and P. D. M. Taylor, 313–26. Toronto: Canadian Scholars Press, 1990.

———. "Migration, Schooling and the Politics of Identity: A Case Study of Caribbean students in a Toronto High School." Master's thesis, York University (Toronto), 1991.

———. "Culture, Schooling and Identity: What Will Be the Focus in the Focus Schools?" Paper presented on a panel entitled *The Educational Experiences of African Canadian Youth*. American Association for African Studies Annual Conference. Toronto, November, 1994.

———. "Identity and Difference in the Caribbean Diaspora: Case Study from Metropolitan Toronto." In *The Reordering of Culture: Latin America, The Caribbean and Canada in the Hood*, ed. Alvina Ruprecht. Ottawa: Carleton University Press, 1995.

Young, Crawford, ed. *Ethnic Diversity and Public Policy: A Comparative Inquiry*. New York: St. Martin's Press, 1998.

Young, Robert J. C. *White Mythologies: Writing, History and the West*. London: Routledge, 1990.

———. *Colonial Desire: Hybridity in Theory, Culture and Race*. New York: Routledge, 1995.

Index

169